MERCY AND HOPE

Mercy and Hope

Mike Pacer

IGNATIUS PRESS
San Francisco, CA

AUGUSTINE INSTITUTE
Greenwood Village, CO

Ignatius Press Distribution
P.O. Box 1339
Fort Collins, CO 80522
Tel: (800) 651-1531
www.ignatius.com

Augustine Institute
6160 S. Syracuse Way, Suite 310
Greenwood Village, CO 80111
Tel: (866) 767-3155
www.augustineinstitute.org

Nihil Obstat: Ryan B. Browning, S.T.L.
Censor Librorum
Imprimatur: + David J. Malloy, D.D., J.C.L., S.T.D.
Bishop of Rockford

Cover Design: Christopher Murphy

ISBN: 978-0-9993756-0-0

Printed in Canada

Contents

PART I—MERCY

PART II—HOPE

Dedication

To my wife, Lori, who introduced me to the message of Divine Mercy and who constantly helps me to grow in hope.

Foreword

We live in a world that sometimes seems more and more broken each day. In the face of a seemingly endless succession of wars, economic collapse, natural disasters, and random acts of violence, many of us find ourselves living with a pervading sense of fear and frustration. Even those of us who are Christians find ourselves struggling to make sense of it all—to truly seek God, to come to terms with our own brokenness and need for mercy, and to find glimmers of hope, questioning whether it's ever going to get any better. This book comes into that space with some powerful and inspiring answers.

The first thing I thought of when Mike Pacer asked me to read his manuscript (which I somehow thought was just a book about mercy) is that there can never be too much written about mercy. Indeed, in spite of radically differing personalities and styles, our last three popes have presented an amazing continuity of teaching, stressing that there is nothing the world needs more than Divine Mercy. It is more powerful than evil; it is the core of the Gospel; it is the most important message that Christ gave us.

When I wrote *7 Secrets of Divine Mercy*, I chose the number 7 as a way of sticking with the theme of the first two books in what is now the "7 Secrets" series. But there are many more "hidden" truths about the nature of God and his Church than the ones I chose to present. Some are in the hearts and minds of mystics and theologians, but unknown to most Catholics; and some remain within the mystery of the Triune God. So there is always more for us to discover! And on our journey to deeper union with God and greater transformation in our lives, we should always be seeking and asking for more, because God really does desire to reveal himself to us, to give us more of his gifts and more of himself.

Every person who speaks or writes on a particular topic tends to bring new insights and a new tone that makes the message hit you differently, because it comes through the filter of a completely unique individual—one who, in this case, has personal experience of everything he's writing about.

Mike Pacer has an extensive background, and I've been blessed to know him and his work for several years. As a trial lawyer in Chicago, he had a deep conversion of heart and went on to get his master's in theology, lead retreats, and start a ministry for parish evangelization and renewal. But his book is not a theological treatise; his writing, like his personality, is real and down-to-earth.

As I read through Part I, I was more and more impressed with how clearly and completely Mike leads us deeper into the reality of God as a perfect Father who did not create us casually, but with a specific purpose. This Father, Mike assures us, is not indifferent to his children's daily struggles, but wants "an ongoing personal relationship with us. God wants to walk with us, speak with us, share our hopes and dreams, bear our burdens and sorrows, guide us, guard us, and lead us to our perfection in Heaven."

What becomes clear as you read on is the all-important reminder that our creation by this Father includes a promised destiny: that, if we say yes to his gift of mercy, God will help us become like him so that we can live with him in perfect and unending joy. As Mike explains, "We are invited to share divine life with God. Our destiny is not the grave, but eternal peace and joy in Heaven.... [We] are destined for glory."

Moving on to Part II, the section on hope, I didn't really know what to expect. (If you'll pardon a bad pun, I didn't know what to hope for.) When I had first realized that this wasn't just a book on mercy, but was split into two roughly equal parts on mercy and hope, I wondered why the two themes were included in one book. How was he going to tie it all together?

But, as it turned out, this was my favorite part of the book, and I can't emphasize enough how important I think hope is for our time. There's so much more than simply knowing about this theological virtue or having some vague sense of hoping for heaven. Mike shows us that hope is a way to live—with happiness, meaning, and purpose to our lives—even in the midst of a world that seems lost in turmoil.

To me, the most wonderful and powerful thing Mike has done in this book is to show us the interconnectedness of mercy and hope. True hope is not just wishful thinking, not just a "pipe dream," not just a sad, empty longing for something that we really don't expect will happen. It's the inner assurance that what we long for will actually be realized!

How do we get the type of hope that Mike talks about in Part II? By understanding and accepting the reality of mercy he tells us about in Part I. Without God's mercy, we can have no hope. Real, life-changing hope comes when I can say, "Yes, Jesus, I trust in You."

No matter what happens to me in the book of my life, trust in God's mercy tells me that he can and will write the last chapter if I let him. If I trust that he really does love me in spite of my unworthiness, that he really has gone before me to prepare a place for me (cf. Jn 14:3), that he really can "turn all things to good for those who love him" (Rom 8:28), then I can live in the sure hope that he will fulfill for me the promise he gave his disciples: "I will see you again and your hearts will rejoice, and no one will take your joy from you" (Jn 16:22).

Vinny Flynn
Founder of MercySong Ministries of Healing
Author of *7 Secrets of Divine Mercy*
Stockbridge, MA

Preface

It is surprising to me that I felt called to write a book on mercy and hope. I have struggled to receive God's mercy and to embrace the reality that God loves me in spite of my many sins. I have lacked hope, unable to readily accept the fact that God has prepared a place for me in Heaven and that he yearns for me to be with him despite my unworthiness. This book does not impart the pearls of spiritual wisdom of a great saint. Rather, it shares the insights of an ordinary Catholic who has struggled to accept God's mercy and to live in hope.

I have always had faith in God. But this was not enough. I believed in God's existence. I believed in the infallibility of the Bible. I believed in the teachings of the Church. Yet I still often felt empty, unworthy, and hopeless. I loved God and often felt his love. But even this was not enough. Those feelings of love came and went. When they left, I often felt ugly, unlovable, and hopeless. Then I was introduced to the message of Divine Mercy imparted to St. Faustina by Our Lord. This, coupled with my faith in and love for God, was finally enough.

In the message of Divine Mercy, I began to see more clearly the infinite, perfect, personal love of God for me revealed in his merciful nature. God is always merciful. He is always forgiving. He is always loving. Nothing I do will ever change that. This is not to deny my freedom to reject his love. But I can do nothing to stop God from loving me.

For me, the message of Divine Mercy was a gateway to understanding the breadth of God's mercy, revealed not just to a saintly nun in the twentieth century, but to all mankind throughout history. I saw the mercy of God revealed in creation, in the law given to Moses, in the trials and sufferings of God's people. I saw mercy in the Incarnation, in the example of Jesus, in his teachings, and in Jesus's suffering, Death, and Resurrection.

Most important in my journey to understand mercy was the realization that God's mercy is personal. God is not merciful in some general, theological sense. God's mercy is not for "us." God's mercy is for me. And God does not reserve his mercy for me only if I achieve a certain level of sanctity or avoid a certain amount of sin. God's mercy is not offered to the "me" I wish I could be, but the very "me" that I am. God's mercy is for the "me" that is full of sin and imperfections. His mercy is for the "me" that runs from him in one way or another on a daily basis. I do not and cannot merit God's mercy. Yet it is freely offered to me at all times.

This reality of God's infinite personal mercy became the basis for my ever-growing hope. Never in my life have I been "good enough" to deserve God's love or the perfection of Heaven. This reality has not changed. But my understanding of this truth has changed dramatically. I will never be "good enough" to attain heaven. I will never have to be. Hope is the realistic expectation that I will be in Heaven with God for all eternity, not because I deserve it, but because I ask for it and because God gives it to me.

My journey to understand and embrace hope brought me to the realization that, like mercy, all of salvation history testifies to the hope found in God. Both the Old and New Testament reveal the hard truth that my true happiness and fulfillment are not found here on earth. Even the very best that creation has to offer will always fall short of fully satisfying me. On my own, I will never truly find happiness. But, while revealing this truth, the Bible also imparts hope. The Bible fills me with the hope that one day I will be fully satisfied. One day I will experience not mere transitory physical or emotional happiness, but true, unending, soulful joy.

The Old Testament hints at the reason for hope and the New Testament clearly reveals the reason for hope. The reason for hope is Jesus Christ. In Jesus, God shows that he loves me so much that he emptied himself of his glory, became a man like me, suffered, died, and rose for me. Because of Jesus, I need never doubt God's love or mercy. Because of Jesus, I need never doubt my worth in God's eyes. Because of Jesus, I need not fear death. Because of Jesus, I can be sure of my ultimate eternal destination—perfect peace and joy in community with God, the angels, and my brothers and sisters in Heaven. Jesus spoke words of hope. He lived the example of hope. And through his life, Death, and Resurrection, he imparted to me the reality that I always have reason for hope.

Hope is not primarily a feeling, but a decision to trust in God. Hope is a decision to trust the God that created me in love, sustains me in love and has promised me his gift of infinite, eternal love. It is a decision to trust that God will do exactly as he has always promised—to shower me with love and mercy, both here on earth and in heaven.

As I sought to embrace God's mercy, it became clear to me that God's mercy and the theological virtue of hope are intimately connected. In fact, they are inseparable. God's mercy is the cause for my hope. Even the words our Lord requested to be written on the Image of Divine Mercy, "Jesus, I trust in You," are words of mercy and hope. When I say these words, I am in effect saying, "Jesus, I hope in your mercy."

Along my spiritual journey, I came to the realization that one of the surest ways to come to embrace mercy and hope is through Mary. Mary is literally the "Mother of Mercy," in that she is the mother of Jesus, Mercy incarnate. Mary is also literally the "Mother of Hope," as she is the mother of Jesus, Hope incarnate. Mary's life was the greatest human example of both mercy and hope. She trusted completely in God's plan. Her "yes" to God was a complete gift of herself to all of us and a free assent to God's gift of her Son to all of us. As my mother, Mary constantly intercedes on our behalf to her Son that he pour out his mercy and hope upon me.

I pray that this book will draw you near to the merciful Heart of Jesus and fill you with great hope.

Mike Pacer

Solemnity of All Saints, 2017

PART I

MERCY

ONE

Mercy Defined

What Is Mercy?

Perhaps you were the child who didn't heed your mom's warning to stop roughhousing, and broke a window. Your exuberance turned to sorrow, shame, and fear. But when your father got home, he picked you up, wiped away your tears, and said, "I forgive you." Perhaps you were the teenager whose teacher took a personal interest in you, assured you of your potential, and greatly encouraged you. Maybe a neighbor gave you a bicycle that her son or daughter had outgrown, or a stranger gave you tickets to take your son to the game. Maybe your boss gave you a second chance when you failed to close the big deal, or your spouse forgave you for unfaithfulness. Or maybe you have simply been the recipient of a kind word or a kind gesture from a stranger.

If you have ever experienced any of the situations above or any other similar experience, you have experienced mercy. Most of us, if not all of us, have experienced mercy, and therefore have an innate understanding of it. But none of us can fathom the depths of mercy we have received. We can hardly recognize the amount of mercy shown to us daily by our fellow man; so when it comes to God's mercy toward us, we tend to be downright oblivious. The goal of this book is to wake us up and stir our hearts with a new realization of God's great love and mercy.

Lest we try to run before we walk, we will start by considering a simple definition of mercy. Mercy is commonly defined as: (a) forgiveness of the offender by the offended or (b) as compassion given/shown to one who does not necessarily merit such compassion. While these definitions fall woefully short of communicating the depth of what we shall come to understand as mercy, nonetheless, they are a good place to start.

Everyone, even those who profess no particular creed or code, can readily admit that to be human is to be imperfect. Each of us has been mean, rude, or disrespectful to another. Each of us has spread a rumor, lied, or cheated another. And each of these acts has unjustly hurt another.

In addition to the intentional harm that we might inflict on others, we can also unintentionally cause injury through negligence. You might have forgotten the milk because you failed to write it on the shopping list. You might have underbid the job because you failed to double-check your figures. You might have missed your child's recital because you got too caught up in work and lost track of time. Regardless of what you might have intended, in each of these situations your actions caused someone else pain.

What was the result of these intentional or unintentional wrongs? Fortunately, your child didn't run away from home because you missed his or her recital or because you served toast instead of cereal. Fortunately, your mother didn't

disown you for your disrespectfulness. Your friendship sur-
vived a "betrayal," and your spouse didn't get even for your
lie by hiding your car keys. Instead, each of these people was
merciful and forgave you.

The mercy we receive through explicit or silent forgiveness
is complemented by the mercy shown to us through the
compassion of others. Maybe we were taught by an enthusiastic
Scout leader or treated by an empathetic nurse. We have
walked through gardens planted by generous volunteers
and driven though neighborhoods illuminated by Christmas
lights. We have received countless birthday wishes, invitations
to lunch or dinner, and words of condolence for the loss of a
loved one. Every day, we experience a smile, a kind word, or
maybe even a compliment. Everywhere we turn, we see mercy
extended by our friends, family, and even strangers.

Our lives are inundated with the mercy shown to us by
others. And yet this mercy is but a faint reflection of the
infinite, overwhelming mercy that we will soon realize comes
from God.

Infinitely Inequitable Mercy

The depth of mercy extended in each situation is revealed by
the relationship between the giver and the receiver and by the
nature of a merciful act. Conversing with and giving money
to a beggar is more merciful than purchasing a lunch for a
good friend because nothing is *owed* to the beggar, there is no
chance of repayment, and it is uncomfortable to stoop down
and talk to someone whose plight makes us uneasy. Greater
mercy is shown by a mother who mows the grass when her

son forgets to on prom weekend than by the son who mows it as his regular chore. It's easier for the son to mow the grass, and his act is more an act of justice than mercy because of everything he receives from his mother.

Now let us try to imagine the mercy of God. It is merciful for you to forgive a friend who gossips about you or to give your coat to a homeless man. It is even more merciful to forgive an unfaithful spouse or to devote every Friday night to working in a homeless shelter. It is heroically merciful to forgive someone who has murdered your child or to sell everything you have and work as a missionary. But God has not given us a coat, some food, or forty years of service. God has given us life, the earth, our families and friends, and the potential for eternal joy in Heaven.

God does not merely offer to forgive us for all the times we ignore him, take his name in vain, and negligently hurt one of his other sons or daughters. God offers to forgive us for every thought, word, action, and omission that we have committed against him, ourselves, and our neighbor. God is so merciful that he lowered himself, becoming man, in order to suffer and die in reparation for every sin that would ever be committed by all mankind.

All of creation is a pure gift from God. He is so loving and so merciful that his love and mercy cannot be contained; he created us so that he could give us every good gift, especially his very own divine life, for all eternity. There is nothing we have done or could ever do to merit our lives and the innumerable blessings God has bestowed upon us. And yet, he desires to share unceasingly his love and bestow his mercy on all.

God completely transcends his creation, yet mercifully offers us intimacy with him. Imagine yourself stooping to pick up an earthworm washed onto the sidewalk and returning it to the soil. That image is nothing compared to God's mercy toward us. God transcends us more than we transcend the worm, and yet to God we are not worms but beloved children!

God reaches down with the love of a perfect Father to embrace us and to be in an ongoing personal relationship with us. God wants to walk with us, speak with us, share our hopes and dreams, bear our burdens and sorrows, guide us, guard us, and lead us to our perfection in Heaven. Jesus tells us that God would not be satisfied with ninety-nine out of a hundred of us embracing his mercy. Rather, he would leave the ninety-nine and seek the one who strayed. If that one was willing, God would not merely lead the strayed sheep back but lift it up on his shoulders, rejoicing in its return (cf. Lk 15:1–7)! Such is the love of God! Such is his mercy!

God's love and mercy are seen in his gift of free will. We, the creatures, are given the power by our Creator to accept or reject anything and everything he desires to give us, even eternal life and joy. God gives us all that is good but forces nothing upon us. He expects nothing from us but desires everything for us. God is so merciful that no matter how many times we reject his gifts, he never ceases to offer them. No matter how many times we wrong him, he never ceases to offer us forgiveness.

For us to forgive even a terrible wrong done to us by a neighbor is noble, but it pales in comparison to God's forgiveness. God created us and sustains us. We owe everything to him. But every day we "do God wrong." We ignore him and

TWO

God's Mercy in the Old Testament

Created in Mercy

God wasn't bored. He didn't need to create us or our world. The created world is not God's Lego set. God doesn't sit on a couch with a bowl of popcorn and watch us for entertainment, although it would be the ultimate reality show.

Perhaps we imagine God as a lonely old man in the clouds, but nothing could be further from the truth. God is eternally a Trinity of Persons—Father, Son, and Holy Spirit. God is the perfect lover, the perfect receiver of love, and the perfect flow of love between the giver and receiver. God is the perfect community, the perfect family. Nothing is lacking in God that would cause him to look outside himself. God is complete and needs nothing. He did not *need* to create us. And yet, he did. So why did God create us? Because God is both love and mercy.

If it were possible to separate perfect love from perfect mercy, then it would seem there was no reason for God to create us because the perfect love of God is expressed fully in the love of the Trinity. In the Trinity we find the lover, the beloved, and the act of love. That God doesn't need us to be Love can be seen in the fact that we were created and are not eternal. Since we did not always exist, we cannot be the recipients of love by which God is defined as lover. Otherwise, before our creation, God would not have been Love.

But perfect love is perfectly generous. It cannot be contained. The perfect love of God is such that God chooses to love that which is undeserving of his love. That is, God loves us who are completely unworthy of his love. This is the mercy of God.

In justice, God was fulfilled in love without creating us. It is perfectly just for the Father to love the Son and the Son to reciprocate that love. The Son deserves the love of the Father and the Father deserves the love of the Son. And both perfectly love each other. But God is both just and merciful. Therefore, in mercy, God created us to share in his love.

God created us who did not deserve to receive his love. We owe everything to God. God deserves our love. But we have done nothing for God so as to deserve his love. This means that God's love for us is pure gift, pure mercy. But it goes even deeper than this. We cannot come close to understanding the mercy of God revealed in creation without taking into account the fall of man.

In the story of creation, we learn that God created everything for our benefit. God gave us the earth and all creatures to serve us and provide for our needs. God created man and woman in his own image to complete each other and to live in harmony with each other and with him. And since God is omniscient, God knew what would happen. God knew that

Adam and Eve would reject his love. God knew that each of us would do the same over and over again. Yet, in mercy, God created us anyway.

Imagine if you had a crystal ball that could see into the future, allowing you to see the result of leaving your teenage son home alone for the weekend while the rest of the family visited Grandma. Imagine you saw the cases of beer being carried in and the party taking place. Imagine you saw kids smoking out on the deck and throwing trash on the neighbor's lawn as they left. Armed with this foreknowledge, you certainly wouldn't leave your son home alone. Yet God, intimately aware of all our faults and failings in advance, allows us to go ahead and sin against ourselves, against our neighbors, and against him.

In love, God gives us free will to choose good or evil. In mercy, God gives us this choice, knowing that we will often choose evil and that he will always forgive us when we repent. In love, God allows us the ability to reject him. In mercy, God allows this choice, knowing that we will often reject him and that he will always welcome us back.

The story of creation in the Book of Genesis is both a love story and a story of mercy. Too often we focus on the fall of man as the end of the Biblical story of creation. God created us in his image and likeness. In love, he gave us everything, but we rejected him. After the Fall, we suffered from the consequences of Original Sin: separation from God, a weakened intellect and will, and subjection to suffering and death. But the fall of man is not the end of the story of creation but a new beginning. God did not withdraw his life of love; rather, he began his outpouring of mercy.

Adam and Eve rejected the wonderful, unmerited gifts God gave them: intimate knowledge of God, knowledge of all things in creation, and freedom from suffering and death. However, they coveted the one thing they could not have as creatures—equality with God. The first man and woman were not satisfied being the pinnacle of creation; instead, they wished to be gods themselves. Because of this desire, God justly "punished" them. That is, he allowed them to experience life without his supernatural, life-giving gifts. Since Adam and Eve refused to cooperate with God's creation as intended, God pronounced that they would struggle against a broken creation:

> Cursed is the ground because of you! In toil you shall eat its yield all the days of your life. Thorns and thistles it shall bear for you, and you shall eat the grass of the field. By the sweat of your brow you shall eat bread, until you return to the ground, from which you were taken; For you are dust, and to dust you shall return. (Gn 3:17–19)

At the very moment that God pronounced his just sentence upon mankind, God also revealed his unfathomable mercy with the following words:

> Then the LORD God said to the snake, … I will put enmity between you and the woman, and between your offspring and hers; they will strike at your head, while you strike at their heel. (Gn 3:14–15)

This passage is referred to as the *protoevangelium*, or "the first gospel," because it reveals the Good News of salvation. Through a man and a woman—Adam and Eve—sin and death entered creation, and Satan was given reign over the world. And, through a man and a woman—Jesus, the new Adam, and Mary, the new Eve—Satan's reign would end, along with our subjection to sin, suffering, and death.

Although Adam and Eve had lost their original gifts, God promised new, eternally better gifts to come. He promised to create a new woman, Mary, who would conform herself perfectly to God's will. He also promised that his own Son, born of Mary, would pay the debt of sin; and that at the end of time he would recreate the world and give us minds that would never be clouded, wills that would never be distorted, and bodies that would neither suffer nor die.

Creation is the overture of mercy that finds its finale in the *Exsultet* sung at the Easter Vigil: "O truly necessary sin of Adam, destroyed completely by the Death of Christ! O happy fault that earned for us so great, so glorious a Redeemer!" The Fall was not the end, but rather the beginning. The sin of mankind resulted not in damnation, but in forgiveness and eternal reward. A life of friendship with God was fulfilled in a perfect, joyful union with God. A life where man arrogantly sought to reach up and make himself a god was substituted by a life in which God humbly reached down and became one of us.

Before he created us, God knew that we would turn away from him and choose to love things other than him. Before he gave us everything we have, he knew we would often choose to worship the gift and deny the giver. Yet still he created us. Why? Because God is mercy. God knew we would harden our hearts. He knew we would withdraw our love for him. And he knew that he would forgive us. Thus, it is appropriate to say that we were created to receive his mercy.

A Merciful Old Testament God

It is a common misconception that the "God of the Old Testament" is a mean and vengeful God, constantly smiting people for their sins, whereas the "God of the New Testament" is a kind and loving Jesus. This perception is wrong on so many levels. First, God is by definition eternally constant; he does not evolve or change. God was both just and merciful in the Old Testament, and he is both merciful and just in the New Testament. Second, it makes no sense to believe an infinite, almighty, loving God is mean or vengeful toward us. To do so suggests that God resembles a child who built some little Lego figures, had a temper tantrum, and then smashed them.

It is true that God's justice is revealed in the Old Testament. When God's people made bad choices, bad things happened to them: Adam and Eve were banished from the Garden of Eden for their disobedience; the waters of the Flood claimed the lives of evildoers; and the Israelites who failed to trust that God would give them the Promised Land wandered in the desert for forty years, died, and never entered it. There are even a few stories in the Old Testament where God is portrayed as "smiting" someone, such as Lot's wife. There are many biblical commentaries, however, that discuss these passages and provide a proper understanding of the justice of God and his "punishments." Without examining them in depth, it is important to have at least a basic understanding of these acts of justice in our journey toward a better understanding of God's mercy.

God is just. Therefore, the world he created contains his justice. In love, God gave us free will to act for or against our own good, and through justice (as well as love), we will reap what we sow. Adam and Eve chose banishment from the Garden by choosing not to live in harmony with God. The people who drowned in the Flood were "corrupt, lawless, depraved and had nothing but evil in their hearts," while Noah and his family were saved because they were "good and blameless" (Gn 7:5–13). After being miraculously freed from Egyptian slavery and brought to the Promised Land, many of the Israelite leaders did not trust God to protect them from its inhabitants, so God let them wander for forty years until they died. Those who did trust God, however, entered the Promised Land. Lot's wife was not willing to completely let go of the evils of Sodom, and so she was turned into a block of salt. The people who chose evil were given evil, and the people who chose good were given good.

The justice seen in the Old Testament continues today. Temporally, if we choose to jump off a building, God will let us fall to our deaths. If we choose to eat unhealthily and never exercise, we will have bad health. Spiritually, if we choose evil—that is, to be separated from God throughout our lives— God will allow us to have such separation both here on earth and for all eternity.

The Old Testament, however, reveals not only God's justice but also his mercy, and to a greater extent. The Old Testament tells us that God is "merciful and gracious, slow to anger and abounding in steadfast love and faithfulness" (Ex 34:6). He is "a kind merciful God" (Dt 4:3), "a gracious and merciful God"

(Neh 9:31), and "compassionate and merciful; he forgives sins and saves in time of distress" (Sir 2:11). We are reminded throughout the Old Testament that God does not wish to punish but to forgive the repentant sinner: "I will not remain angry with you for I am merciful" (Jer 3:12). "I have loved you with an age-old love so I have kept my mercy toward you" (Jer 31:3). "How great is the mercy of the Lord, his forgiveness for those who return to him" (Sir 17:29). And "Let the wicked forsake their way, and the unrighteous their thoughts; let them return to the Lord, that he may have mercy on them, and to our God, for he will abundantly pardon" (Is 55:7). It is further revealed in the Old Testament that, when compared to his justice, God's mercy is infinitely greater: "The Lord will punish to the third and fourth generation, but he will forgive for a thousand generations" (Ex 34:7). This truth will be become abundantly clear in the section of this chapter entitled "God's Mercy for His Unfaithful Spouse."

In his encyclical *Dives in Misericordia*, St. John Paul the Great succinctly illuminates the mercy of God seen in the Old Testament by highlighting the Hebrew words used to describe it. God's mercy is both (1) *hesed*, which means to show goodness, faithfulness, grace, and love, and (2) *rahamin,* a completely gratuitous and unmerited exigency of the heart, both tender and understanding, like that of a mother for the child that springs from her womb. Other Hebrew words used to describe God's mercy include the concepts of pity, compassion, fidelity, solidity, sparing an enemy, and remitting guilt.[1] This is

---

[1]   John Paul II, *Dives in misericordia* (November 30, 1980), note 52.

our God as revealed in the Old Testament: He is good, faithful, loving, tender, understanding, compassionate, and forgiving.

Mercy in the Law

Misunderstanding Scripture can lead us to vilify wrongly the Law written in the Old Testament. Most of us, at some point in our faith journey, were led to believe that Jesus replaced a burdensome, legalistic system of pedantic rules found in the Old Testament with the simple advice to "love." Yet Jesus himself said the exact opposite:

> Do not think that I have come to abolish the law or the prophets. I have come not to abolish but to fulfill. Amen, I say to you, until heaven and earth pass away, not the smallest letter or the smallest part of a letter will pass from the law, until all things have taken place. Therefore, whoever breaks one of the least of these commandments and teaches others to do so will be called least in the kingdom of heaven. But whoever obeys and teaches these commandments will be called greatest in the kingdom of heaven. (Mt 5:17–19)

So, what is the Law, and how could it possibly be "merciful"?

When people familiar with the Old Testament speak of the Law, they are generally referring to the 613 decrees found in the first five books of the Bible, also called the Torah. These decrees range from very profound commands, like "you shall not kill," to practical rules, such as how to diagnose and segregate lepers, and prescriptions for ritual worship. At first, 613 rules might seem excessive, but, compared to the innumerable federal, state, county, and municipal statutes enacted in the United States today, 613 individual prescriptions seem like nothing. It is true, however, that over time various other laws arose by custom and were championed by many leaders of the people. These other laws were attempts to further clarify the prescriptions of the Torah. Anyone familiar with the countless interpretations of laws contained in state and federal appellate court decisions will undoubtedly find the development of Torah prescriptions very familiar.

Since many of us are not Scripture scholars, we have only a general awareness of the existence of these 613 rules. Typically, the Law of the Old Testament for us is the Ten Commandments. Interestingly, most scholars of the Law (both Jewish and Christian) think that all other laws can be categorized under one of the Ten Commandments. So, in effect, the Ten Commandments *are* the Law of the Old Testament. Regardless of whether we are talking about ten sublime truths or hundreds of specific provisions, the Law was not a burden placed on us by God, but a merciful gift.

When we were children, we might have thought that our mothers wanted to torture us when they made us eat our vegetables, or that our fathers wanted to ruin our lives when they told us to turn off the video game and go to sleep. But, we were wrong. Our parents set these rules for us because they loved us. They wanted what was truly best for us. They wanted us to be happy, not for the moment, but for the rest of our lives. In giving us the Law, God gave us the tools to be happy—truly happy—not for a day or even our lifetimes, but for eternity.

At the time the Law was given to Moses on Mt. Sinai, God's people were spiritual "children." They had been raised with stories of creation, the Flood, and God's interaction with the patriarchs Noah, Abraham, Isaac, Jacob, and Joseph. Yet they had no real understanding of God. They had a general concept that they were special to God but no practical way of entering into relationship with God or organized way of worshiping him.

It is also important to understand the other belief systems that surrounded the Israelites. These other religions depicted gods who were separate from and generally disinterested in mankind. Worship was merely a way of trying to appease the gods or swaying a god to act with some favor. None of these gods, however, actually loved mankind. It was at this time of spiritual infancy that God led his people away from these false forms of worship and into the desert where he personally cared for and instructed them. It was at this point that God gave his people the Law.

When Moses read the Law to the people, he exclaimed:

> Behold, I have taught you statutes and ordinances, as the LORD my God commanded me, that you should do them in the land which you are entering to take possession of it. Keep them and do them; for that will be your wisdom and your understanding in the sight of the peoples, who, when they hear all these statutes, will say, "Surely this great nation is a wise and understanding people." For what great nation is there that has a god so near to it as the LORD our God is to us, whenever we call upon him? And what great nation is there, that has statutes and ordinances so righteous as all this law which I set before you this day? (Dt 4:5–8)

From this exclamation, we see that the Law was not imposed upon the people but given as a gift, whose reception engendered gratitude and pride.

This Biblical event, which details the giving of the Law to the Israelites, is referred to as the *Great Theophany*, a phrase that highlights the most important aspect of the event—the manifestation of God himself to his people. The formal title of the Ten Commandments is the *Decalogue*, which is derived from the Greek word meaning "ten words." At the Great Theophany, God manifested himself and gave his people these ten commands, etched in stone, which were placed in the Ark of the Covenant so that God's words would literally dwell with his people.

At the very moment that Moses was receiving the Law from God, the Israelites were involved in an act that clearly demonstrated their need for it. They had grown impatient waiting for Moses to descend from Mt. Sinai and decided to craft an idol to worship instead of the one true God. They gathered their gold and molded a golden calf; and they bowed down before it, offered it sacrifice, and sang, danced, and reveled.

When Moses returned and saw this act of idolatry, he smashed the stone tablets in anger. This was the greatest punishment possible—the loss of the Law.[2] By smashing the tablets, Moses demonstrated that the Israelites had betrayed God and didn't deserve to have God's words or his Law. They had chosen to separate themselves from God and, in justice, deserved the consequences of this choice.

So what was God's response? It was that of a loving and merciful Father. God didn't give up on his people; he didn't

---

[2] Cf. *The Navarre Bible Pentateuch*, notes for Ex 32:15–24, 2000 ed.

leave them on their own to figure it out. Rather, he called Moses back up to Mt. Sinai and gave him the Law again. Moses, having the renewed tablets of the Law, pronounced God's mercy upon the people: "The LORD, the LORD, a God gracious and merciful, slow to anger and abounding in love and fidelity, continuing his love for a thousand generations, and forgiving wickedness, rebellion, and sin" (Ex 34:6–7). This mercy of God surrounds the gift of the Law. When his people were steeped in sin and deserved punishment, he extended mercy.

Through the Law, God gives us instructions on how to enter into a personal relationship with him. He gives us rules of conduct for those times when we find ourselves too weak or too ignorant to determine right conduct. When we lose our way, God gives us directions back to his heart. St. John the Apostle assures us that if we wish to know God and be in union with him, we must keep his commandments: "Whoever says, 'I know him,' but does not keep his commandments is a liar, and the truth is not in him. But whoever keeps his word, the love of God is truly perfected in him" (1 Jn 2:4–5).

God's law can be tough as it challenges us to be like him— even more so under the prescriptions of the New Testament. As does the Old Testament, Jesus admonishes us to love God with our whole heart, mind, and strength. He challenges us to love our neighbor as ourselves. But he also commands us to pray for those who hate us and to forgive all those who wrong us. And Jesus challenges us to "be perfect, just as your heavenly Father is perfect" (Mt 5:48).

We must remember that God's law is not for him, but for us. It is not a test, but a blueprint for eternal happiness. God is a loving Father who wants what is best for his beloved children. As a loving father, God gives us rules to follow for our own good when we are unable to recognize what is best for us. God's mercy is seen in his creation of these rules, and in forgiving us when we fail to act rightly and come to him for forgiveness.

In giving us the law, God in effect is saying to each of us:

> *My beloved child, long before I gave you my law, I gave you freedom. You may choose to follow or disobey my law. But know that in choosing to disobey my law, you choose that which is not of me. And in doing so, you choose that which is not of you because you are a reflection of me. I give you my law so that, if you choose to be with me, you may more easily find the way. I know that you want to love me. But, despite this, you will not always act out of love for me. Therefore, I assure you that for each letter of the law you may break, I possess a corresponding volume of mercy to shower upon you.*

God's Mercy for His Unfaithful Spouse

The Old Testament is an incredible love story. It is a story of a God who loves his people with a love of special choosing, like that of a spouse.[3] He chooses his people to be his "bride." He woos them. He proposes to them, offering to be their God and for them to be his people. Then he waits for their answer. When they say "yes," God acts magnanimously on their behalf, freeing them from captivity, feeding them,

---

[3] This is a phrase especially dear to St. John Paul II. Cf. John Paul II, *Dives in misericordia*, no. 4.

caring for them, and working miracle after miracle for them. He blesses his faithful spouse with land, crops, livestock, and progeny.

Despite all God did for his people in the Old Testament, they were continually unfaithful. They took God for granted, and they turned their backs on him. They ignored his law, and they worshiped other gods. In response to their unfaithfulness, God revealed his tremendous mercy. God never ceased to love his people. He never ceased to call them back to him. He was always willing to be their God, even though they continually chose not to be his people.

This love story of God and his people begins in earnest with Abraham. After Noah's descendants rebelled against God, they were scattered over the earth and, in time, forgot about God completely. But God called Abraham, a descendant of Noah, to found a great nation to which God would bind himself in a covenantal relationship (in effect marrying his people). And God promised that this covenantal relationship would never end.

At God's request, Abraham took his household and left his land, his people, and everything he knew to journey toward an unknown destination of God's choosing. Abraham did so on the assurance that God would bless him and settle him in a new land. He trusted that God would form a great nation from his descendants, and that they would be God's own people. Abraham, for the most part, was faithful to God, trusting him and doing whatever he asked. In response, God was not merely faithful, but rich in generosity. He led Abraham safely to a new and fertile land, he gave him victory over his enemies, and he gave Abraham a son when he and his wife were far beyond the age to have children.

From Abraham's son Isaac sprung the entire nation of Israel and, ultimately, our Lord, Jesus Christ. Unfortunately, between the time of Abraham and Jesus, God's people were often unfaithful with disastrous results. But it is within this setting that the love story of God for his people begins to unfold.

The tremendous mercy of God is exemplified in the story of the Exodus, when God freed the Israelites from their captivity in Egypt through a series of miraculous interventions. First, God sent twelve plagues upon the Egyptians. Then he parted the Red Sea so that the Israelites could escape the pursuing Egyptian army. When they were hungry and thirsty, God miraculously provided them with water, sent quail, which covered the camp in the evening, and gave them bread from Heaven (manna), which covered the ground in the morning. He wooed them with the promise of a land "flowing with milk and honey." He led them when they were lost, healed them when they were sick, and gave them victory over all the people who opposed them.

What a merciful God we see in the Exodus! Yet nothing God did was ever enough for his people. They complained against him. They doubted him. They rebelled against his chosen leader Moses. They constantly refused to do what God asked of them. Even when they stood at the very border of the Promised Land, they refused to enter it, disbelieving that God would give them victory over its inhabitants. But God never gave up on them. He never withdrew his love. He always forgave them.

When the Israelites finally trusted God to deliver them to the Promised Land, he miraculously intervened and gave them victories over all of its unruly inhabitants. They took possession of the lands, settled down, and were blessed with crops, livestock, and children. Then they forgot all about God.

Growing fat and lazy in the Promised Land, the Israelites lost their identity, and began to marry the local inhabitants and worship their false gods instead of the one true God. This resulted in their capture by the king of Mesopotamia. Finding themselves once again enslaved, they called out to the Lord whom they had previously forsaken. And, once again, in his mercy, God answered their prayers. God sent his judge Othni-el to raise an army and free them (cf. Jgs 3:1–11).

Once free, however, they soon turned against the Lord and were defeated by the king of Moab. In his great mercy, God heard their cries for help and sent his judge Ehud to kill the king and lead the people to victory over the Moabites (cf. Jgs 3:12–30). But, of course, the story did not end here.

Upon the death of Ehud, the people turned away from the Lord—again. This time, it was the Canaanites who defeated them. Finding themselves cruelly oppressed, the people again cried to the Lord for help. This time God raised up a female judge, Deborah, to lead the people in revolt and win back their freedom.

How desirable it would have been for this pattern to end with Deborah, but unfortunately it did not. The people turned from God again, and so he sent Gideon to free them from the Midianites and the Amalekites; and again, and so he sent Jephthah to free them from the Ammonites; and yet again, and so God sent Samson to free them from the Philistines. This beautiful dialogue between God and his people perfectly summarizes the period of the Judges:

> Then the Israelites cried out to the LORD, "We have sinned against you, for we have abandoned our God and served the Baals." The LORD answered the Israelites: Did not the Egyptians, the Amorites, the Ammonites, the Philistines, the Sidonians, the Amalekites, and the Midianites oppress you? Yet when you cried out to me, and I saved you from their power, you still abandoned me and served other gods. Therefore I will save you no more. Go and cry out to the gods you have chosen; let them save you in your time of distress. But the Israelites said to the LORD, "We have sinned. Do to us whatever is good in your sight. Only deliver us this day!" And they cast out the foreign gods from their midst and served the LORD, so that he grieved over the misery of Israel (Jgs 10:10–16).

The love story of God and his fickle people continued from the time of the judges into the era of the kings. The people's hearts wandered from God time and time again. Desiring to be like their pagan neighbors, they asked for a king to be appointed to rule over them. In choosing a man rather than God to be their king, they exhibited the same unfaithfulness as their ancestors in the desert. God warned them of the consequences that would result from having a king, but the people were obstinate, and so God granted their request (cf. 1 Sm 8).

From that point onward, the people's fates became intertwined with the actions of the kings. Generally, the kings (and thus the people) went from good, to bad, to worse. King David, who truly loved the Lord, fell into great sin but repented. Thus, his kingdom flourished. David's son Solomon began well but then took numerous pagan wives and concubines and began worshiping their gods. Following Solomon's lead, pagan worship became rampant in the kingdom.

As a result of their betrayal, the unity of God's people was fractured, and the people were split into two kingdoms. The Northern kings were particularly wicked and their people particularly unfaithful. As a result, they were ultimately defeated by the Assyrians, who carried them off into exile. Thus, they ceased to exist as a people.

The Southern kings and their people weren't much better, but there was always a small remnant who remained faithful. At the height of their unfaithfulness, however, the Southern Kingdom was defeated and exiled by the Babylonians. Yet God, out of faithfulness and mercy, did not forsake his people; instead, he continually inspired prophets to lead his people back to him. Finally, when their hearts had softened and they repented of their unfaithfulness, God brought his people back to Jerusalem, where the Temple and true worship of the Lord were restored.

This theme of God's incredible mercy for his people, which underlies the entire Old Testament, is pointedly represented in the Book of Hosea. Hosea married Gomer, knowing that she would be an unfaithful harlot. After a short-lived honeymoon, Gomer was, in fact, unfaithful and left Hosea to pursue adulterous affairs. Hosea punished Gomer by withdrawing all that he had given her. Finding herself stripped of everything and ashamed, Gomer repented and returned to Hosea. In return, Hosea not only forgave Gomer but pursued her until he convinced her to forsake her false lovers and return to him forever.

God bound himself to his people through a covenantal relationship, like Hosea to Gomer. And just as Gomer's love for Hosea was short-lived, so too was the Chosen People's love for God. Like Gomer, they were completely unfaithful despite God's steadfast love. And so God punished his people by withdrawing the unmerited favor he had previously showered upon them; a punishment they justly received as the result of their bad choices. But this punishment was limited and helped move their hearts to repentance. It helped to strip them of their pride and selfishness. Naked and without the protection of God, they became aware of their utter need of him. In their shame, they recalled the golden days of their faithfulness and repented. His people returned to their previous love for God and were warmly embraced. This is the love of God. This is his fidelity. This is his mercy.

THREE

Jesus: Mercy Incarnate

For God so loved the world that he gave his only Son,
so that everyone who believes in him might not perish
but might have eternal life. For God did not send his
Son into the world to condemn the world, but that
the world might be saved through him. (Jn 3:16–17)

The Mercy of the Incarnation

Take a moment to consider why God became "incarnate."[1]
Why would the omnipotent, omniscient, eternal Creator God
set aside his beauty, glory, and infinitude to become man, a
creature constrained by time and space and subject to the will
of evildoers and the experiences of want, deprivation, pain,
and death? Why would God become the very creature that,
from the time of creation, continued to reject him? Because
God *is* mercy! God reveals the depth of his mercy through his
Incarnation and in its effects.

Man and woman were created in the image of God to live
in harmony and joy with him. Because God loves us, he gives

---

[1] *Incarnate* means "to become flesh"; from the Latin *in caro*.

us free will so that we might choose life with him. Yet free will entails the possibility that we might reject God and choose to separate ourselves from him. Adam and Eve chose separation and death. And throughout the Old Testament, we constantly see our ancestors choosing separation and death. Every day we are faced with the choice between good and evil, between what is of God and what is not of God. When we choose that which is not of God, we choose evil and separate ourselves from God. In justice, we deserve the natural result of our choice—eternal separation from God.

God is just, and he is willing to give us a just sentence for our sins. He is willing to let us have exactly what we choose—separation and death. But, he is also merciful, and in his great mercy he does not want us to be separated from him, but to live in joyful union with him for all eternity. This creates a problem: in justice, we deserve death, but in mercy, God wishes to give us life. The Incarnation is the solution to this problem.

In sinning against God, man broke a relationship he could not fix and owed a debt he could not repay. The Incarnation is God becoming fully man, while also remaining fully God. As the second Person of the Blessed Trinity, God assumed a human nature, while also retaining his divine nature. As man, Jesus paid the debt owed by man. As God, Jesus fixed that which only God could fix. God became man to save us *from* the consequences of sin. He became man to save us *for* a new and glorious eternal life with him.

The act of the Incarnation was one of infinite mercy. The Creator became part of creation. The infinite accepted physical constraints. The master became a slave. The Divine became man with all of man's weaknesses. God, who lacks nothing, needed to breathe, eat, and sleep. As man, God felt fatigue, hunger, loneliness, fear, rejection, and loss. God was insulted, slandered, rejected, spit upon, slapped, beaten, scourged, and crucified. And God submitted himself to human death. He did all this for us.

Imagine coming upon a poor beggar covered in sores. Ordinary mercy might compel you to say a kind word or place some money in his cup. Great mercy might compel you to pay for his admittance into a care facility. Heroic mercy, like that exhibited by St. Teresa of Calcutta, might compel you to carry this man home in your arms, bathe him, bandage his wounds, and then place him in your bed and care for him for the rest of his life. But God's infinite mercy compelled God to crawl down into the gutter with the man and embrace him; to remove all of the sores from the man by taking them upon his own flesh; to suffer the man's pain and die in his place; to heal the man far beyond his original state of health; and to lift the man out of the gutter and carry him into the eternal joy of Heaven.

Yet God emptying himself of his divinity to share in our humanity is only half of the act of mercy that is the Incarnation. The second half was stooping down to become man in order that man might become God![2]

As we previously discussed, God creating us to share in his love and life was an act of infinite mercy. Yet God remained,

---

[2] Cf. *CCC*, 460 and quotations from Sts. Irenaeus, Athanasius, and Thomas Aquinas contained in the footnotes thereto.

in a sense, distant from us. He was Creator and we were creature. God was pure, eternal spirit, and we were finite beings possessing a spirit subject to all the flaws of the flesh. We were made in God's image, but not in his divine nature. Though created to share in God's life, we misused our free will and chose death.

Through his Incarnation, however, God obliterated the distance that existed between him and man. Jesus is true God and true man, i.e., one hundred percent God and one hundred percent man. In Jesus, divinity and humanity are perfectly and inseparably joined. In mercy, God became man to experience all that is man: pain, separation, and death. God became man to pay the debt owed by man. God became man not only to reunite that which was separated, but also to join God to man in a new and infinitely more intimate manner.

Through the Incarnation, man received all that was God. In Jesus, man bore perfect love for God and for his fellow man. In Jesus, man was in complete union with God and all creation. In Jesus, man received the full glory of God. In Jesus, man's nature was raised higher than its original state, capable of eternal union with God in Heaven. And in Jesus, God's mercy is extended to all mankind. Through Christ's Death and Resurrection and his sending of the Holy Spirit, we become members of Christ's own Body and communicants in his divine nature.[3] Through the mercy of the Incarnation, we need not merely remain "images of God" as originally

---

[3] See *CCC*, 1988 and the quotation by St. Athanasius in the footnote thereto.

created, but we can share in Christ's nature—the very divine nature of God.

To emphasize even further the great mercy of God in the Incarnation, we must look at its timing, both for mankind in general and for each of us individually. Theoretically, God could have declared, immediately after Adam and Eve repented, that their repentance was sufficient, and he could have restored their natures and welcomed them into Heaven. But he didn't. Rather, God waited until man had rejected him repeatedly and discarded his numerous graces before glorifying mankind. No matter how merciful it would have been for God to glorify man in a state of grace, it was infinitely more merciful to glorify man in a state of sin.

Theoretically, God could whisk each of us to Heaven the first time we are given a choice to sin and choose not to. That would definitely prevent us from choosing to sin and rejecting God the next time we were presented with that choice. But it would not allow God to reveal the true nature of his mercy. He sought not to save the sinless, but to save the sinner. He did not want to elevate merely a photocopy to the level of a masterpiece, but a crumpled and discarded sketch. God wants each of us to know that no sin committed is unforgivable. No matter how far we stray, he will journey the distance and offer to lead us back. There is no lack of love on our part that cannot overwhelmingly be filled with his tender mercy. And no joy imaginable can compare to that which he has in store for us!

As we noted at the beginning of the book, the depth of mercy is revealed in the relationship between the giver and the receiver and in the nature of the act of mercy. Nowhere is this better seen than in the Incarnation. The transcendent Creator God became a lowly creature to save his creatures from the death they had brought upon themselves. And God did so not only to save them from death, but also to elevate them to a glory unattainable prior to sin—a glory by which they would never again choose death, and so would live in the eternal life of God.

Example of Mercy

The life of Jesus is the life of absolute mercy; it is the example par excellence of mercy. In all that he said and did, Jesus exhibited mercy. We have already discussed the mercy expressed through the Incarnation, and we will later discuss the unfathomable mercy exhibited by Jesus in his Passion and Death. But, for now, we will focus on the mercy shown—in both simple and extraordinary ways—by Jesus throughout his life. Mindful of how St. John concludes his Gospel, "The world itself could not contain the books that would be written [concerning Jesus]," we will focus only on a few examples.

The Merciful Wedding Feast. Of all the miracles contained in the Gospels, the story of the Wedding Feast at Cana, found in the second chapter of John, perhaps strikes some people as rather trivial. In this story, while Jesus, his mother Mary, and his disciples attended a wedding, the wine ran out. Mary brought this to the attention of Jesus, who directed the servers to fill six stone jars, each having a twenty to thirty gallon capacity, with water. He then turned the water into wine, whose quality surpassed that of all the wine previously served.

The importance of this miracle cannot be ignored. Given that this is the very first recorded miracle of Jesus, it must be significant. St. John Paul II attested to this by including the story of Cana as one of the five Luminous Mysteries of the Rosary. Two themes are most often stressed regarding this miracle. The first is the illumination of Jesus as God, both in the miraculous nature of the act and in the foreshadowing of the Eucharist (the transubstantiation of wine into the very Blood of Christ). The second is the power of intercessory prayer, especially the special intercessory role of Mary on behalf of us all. But there is another theme of this story—the theme of mercy.

In Jesus's time, weddings were of great cultural importance. Extended family would gather together to celebrate for a prolonged time, generally seven days. Wedding feasts were greatly anticipated breaks from the hardships of everyday life. The wine served at these occasions was an integral part of the celebration, and so it would be a terrible letdown to many if the wine ran out before the celebration ended. It would also be a great embarrassment to the family hosting the wedding.

Weddings were also of great spiritual importance; they signified the covenant between God and his people. Although the miracle at Cana can seem mundane compared to Jesus's healing the blind and the lame and his raising the dead, it is the mundaneness of this miracle that reveals God's great mercy.

In turning the water into wine, Jesus reveals that no concern of ours is beneath God's attention. Mary's motherly concern pierced his heart. At her request alone, Jesus would have poured out his mercy. But the tender heart of Jesus also focused on the bride and the groom, whose life would begin with a failed wedding; and it focused on the family who would bear the shame of letting down so many people. The heart of Jesus blazed with love for his people, and he desired that they should enjoy a brief time of happiness here on earth, a small taste of the eternal wedding banquet that awaited them in Heaven.

No concern of ours is too insignificant to be brought before our merciful Lord. We must bring every perceived need to Jesus. We must share with him all of our hopes and fears. It is an act of love and an act of trust when we share even our smallest concerns with God. Just as Mary made her needs known to Jesus, so should we make our needs known to Jesus. Just as Mary trusted that Jesus would do what was best, so should we. Does this mean that Jesus will answer our every request in the way we expect? No. Jesus loves us far more than that. Jesus's mercy extends far beyond our capacity to know what we need. Jesus will answer all of our prayers in a way far greater than we can imagine.

Merciful Healings. How is it possible that we are not constantly moved to tears at the audacious mercy exhibited by Jesus toward the sick and the suffering? With a word or touch from Jesus, the lame walked, the blind saw, the deaf heard, the mute spoke, the lepers were made clean, and the possessed were delivered from bondage. Have we heard these stories so many times that we have become jaded? Have they lost their intrigue? If so, it is time to read them again, as if for the first time, and to put ourselves into the stories with the sure knowledge that Jesus wants to heal *us*!

Imagine the poor cripple who sat daily near the pool of Bethesda, hoping that one day someone might carry him into the water that was believed to have healing properties (see Jn 5:1–9). Thirty-eight years of illness, longing, loneliness, and despair vanished in an instant with the words of Jesus, "Rise, take up your pallet and walk."

Imagine the woman who was hemorrhaging for twelve years (cf. Lk 8:43–48). She was not only ill, but also destitute because she had spent all of her money seeking a cure. Furthermore, this woman was perceived as "unclean" by her people, and so others feared to touch her. Twelve years of bleeding and twelve years of exile from any tender touch of another person were instantly ended at the mere touch of the fringe of Jesus's garment.

Imagine the great crowds that came to Jesus at the Sea of Galilee, bringing him "the lame, the blind, the deformed, the mute, and many others with various afflictions" (Mt 15:30). Jesus healed them all: the mute spoke, the lame walked, the blind could see, and the maimed were made whole. The prayers of all those who brought their loved ones to Jesus for healing were answered.

Jesus walked among the suffering and the destitute. He immersed himself in the needs and the wants of the people. Faced with the afflictions of others, Jesus was "deeply moved in spirit and troubled" and he "wept" (Jn 11:33–35). The Lord of the universe cried at the plight of his people. The mercy of Jesus is such that he feels every pain we feel.

Are we sick, infirm, lonely, or destitute? Does someone we love suffer? Are they at the point of death? Jesus is intimately concerned with these questions because he is intimately concerned with our plight. He takes our agony upon himself and weeps with us. He begs us to bring our troubles to him and ask for his help. And he will pour out his mercy upon us. Did every person who encountered Jesus receive physical healing? No. Will we receive the exact remedy that we believe we need? Maybe. But will our prayers be heard and answered? Will we receive eternal healing? Yes, without a doubt! Recall the assurance of Jesus:

> Ask and it will be given to you; seek and you will find; knock and the door will be opened to you. For everyone who asks, receives; and the one who seeks, finds; and to the one who knocks, the door will be opened. Which one of you would hand his son a stone when he asks for a loaf of bread or a snake when he asks for a fish? If you then, who are wicked, know how to give good gifts to your children, how much more will your heavenly Father give good things to those who ask him. (Mt 7:7–11)

Mercy toward Sinners. Jesus confirmed what his Father sought to communicate to his people throughout salvation history; that is, no sin is so great that it cannot be forgiven.

Recall the story of the woman caught in adultery (cf. Jn 8:1–11). The leaders of the people brought to Jesus a woman guilty of adultery, a capital offense under the Law. They sought to test Jesus's righteousness. Would he condemn the woman to the just punishment or give her a free pass, which she did not deserve? Jesus did neither. Rather, in justice, Jesus showed great mercy. First, Jesus stayed the hand of the would-be executioners by pointing out that none of them were free of sin, and thus incapable to sit in judgment of others. Jesus did not do this to deny the sin or to deny that serious sin justly deserves punishment. But instead, he poured out his mercy. Jesus said to the woman, "Neither do I condemn you. Go, [and] from now on do not sin anymore." What Jesus meant by these words is that although we have sinned and deserve death, he does not wish us death but new life; he wishes us to recognize our sin, to repent of our sin, and to sin no more.

Recall also the story of the woman who barged into the house of a Pharisee named Simon as Jesus was having dinner there. She prostrated herself at the feet of Jesus, wetting them with her tears and drying them with her hair (cf. Lk 7:38–50). Simon was perturbed by the fact that Jesus allowed this inappropriate behavior; it seemed as if Jesus were unaware that she was a notorious sinner. But Jesus acknowledged his awareness of her sins, saying, "Her sins were many." Knowing that Simon and the others present were scandalized, Jesus chastised them and said to the woman, "Your sins are forgiven.... Your faith has saved you." Jesus was not concerned with the customs that prevented contact with such women. He was not concerned about upsetting his host or the other guests. This woman was in great sin and in need of great healing. Nothing would stand in the way of the mercy that Jesus intended to pour into her soul. This day she would be completely forgiven. This day she would be saved!

We are called to cast ourselves upon the feet of Jesus. We are to admit openly our sins and to acknowledge our need for forgiveness and healing. We must ignore the ridicule that we might encounter because of our faith in Jesus. We must cry out through tears of love for the mercy that we do not deserve.

And our Lord *will* pour out his mercy. He *will* forgive us of all our sins. He *will* heal us. He *will* save us!

Though Christ offered forgiveness to all, not all accepted his offer. He forgave tax collectors, adulterers, and even murderers. Many of those who asked for physical healings received forgiveness of sins, a gift of greater mercy than the physical healings. Curing physical blindness results in a person's ability to see for the rest of his life, but curing the spiritual blindness of sin enables a person to see for all eternity. We must not be afraid to ask for forgiveness of any and all our sins. We must continually seek the mercy of God. And God will grant it to us.

Mercy Greater Than Death. For many, the greatest pain imaginable is the loss of a loved one, especially a child. On two occasions, Jesus showed the great power of his mercy by raising a child from the dead. The first involved the daughter of a synagogue official named Jairus, and the other involved the son of a woman from the town of Nain (cf. Mk 5:21–24, 35–43; Lk 7:11–17).

Picture in your mind Jairus falling at the feet of Jesus, crying and begging Jesus to come and heal his twelve-year-old daughter on the verge of death. Imagine this father's pain and anguish upon arriving home with Jesus only to learn that his little girl had died. Now imagine his great joy when, at Jesus's words, "Little girl, I say to you, arise," his daughter arose from death and walked!

Now call to mind the pitiful scene in Nain. A funeral procession passed in front of Jesus, carrying a young man who had died. The dead man's mother was a widow, and she had no other children. She wept from the depths of her heart because she had lost all that had meaning for her. Jesus touched the funeral bier and said, "Young man, I say to you, arise." After the young man rose from death, Jesus "gave" him back to his mother. It is important to understand that the mercy shown here was for the mother, not her son. She was the one who needed her son. She was the one in despair. And Jesus's concern for this woman was so great that not even death would prevent him from showing mercy toward her.

There is a third biblical account of Jesus raising the dead—the raising of Lazareth. This biblical account gives us a great appreciation of God's mercy. As Lazarus was a very close friend of Jesus, it seems safe to assume that he was a good man, destined for Heaven. Therefore, it was not for Lazarus's sake that Jesus raised him from the dead. Jesus loved Lazarus and was moved to tears at his death. He could have arrived earlier and healed Lazarus, and thus prevented himself from experiencing this sadness. Therefore, Jesus did not raise Lazarus for himself. Nor was it for Martha, who, in her grief, declared her faith in Jesus's divinity and in the ultimate resurrection of her brother in Heaven. So for whom did Jesus perform this miracle? He raised Lazarus from the dead for us, so we would know that despite our frail, sinful condition, we are meant not for death but life.

We all experience pain, and we will all experience physical death. Although Jesus raised them from the dead, Jairus's daughter, the widow's son, and Lazarus all died eventually. Even Jesus, God Incarnate, died on the Cross. If we had perfect hope of the final resurrection, we would presumably not grieve but rejoice in the death of a loved one. But we do not have perfect hope; we are human. To be human is to love, and to love is to grieve the separation of our beloved. But through God's mercy, death is not the end, and all pain will pass away one day. Jesus raised the dead to attest to this ultimate mercy.

Jesus raised these individuals from the dead to give us hope. He demonstrated that God's mercy is greater than any force, even death. Jesus foreshadowed the final and much greater resurrection that we all are offered. Jesus showed that by accepting his mercy, our ultimate end is not death but eternal life with him. Jesus said to Martha, and says to us all, "I am the resurrection and the life; whoever believes in me, even if he dies, will live, and everyone who lives and believes in me will never die" (Jn 11:25).

Teachings of Mercy

In the Gospel of Luke, we learn that Jesus initiated his public ministry by quoting the following words from the prophet Isaiah:

> The Spirit of the Lord is upon me, because he has anointed me to bring glad tidings to the poor. He has sent me to proclaim liberty to captives and recovery of sight to the blind, to let the oppressed go free, and to proclaim a year acceptable to the Lord. (Lk 4:18–19)

These words reveal Jesus's mission to spread mercy to all mankind.

Think of all the proclamations we might have expected Jesus to make in order to emphasize his work here on earth: "I am here to reveal the Trinity and other theological truths of which you are unaware"; "I was sent to point out your many sins"; "Adam and Eve broke creation, and I'm here to fix it"; or maybe, "My Father sent me here to reveal the best way to worship him." While perhaps these phrases seem a bit flippant, we can probably agree that the import of each would be the thesis we might give if we were sent instead of Jesus.

Instead of focusing on our sins, ignorance, or separation from God, Jesus drew attention to the need for mercy. Jesus came to bring good news and hope to the poor—both the materially and spiritually poor. God was aware of their suffering, and wanted them to know that it would come to an end. Jesus came to proclaim liberty to those held in bondage, whether literal or figurative. He wanted to free those unjustly bound in physical chains, as well as those bound emotionally and spiritually. Jesus came to give sight to the blind. He healed not only those who were physically blind, but also those who were blinded by pride, envy, self-righteousness, and despair— if they would listen to his words and embrace his mercy. Jesus also came to promote freedom from all oppression—the oppression of tyranny, false teachings, legalism, and of our fallen nature.

Those of us who are "practicing" Catholics can be much like the people of Jesus's time. We can focus too much on the fact that we give one hour a week to God on Sunday, or that we haven't murdered anyone. Or we might even read the Bible regularly and give money to charity. That's great, but Jesus didn't come to hand out awards. He came to heal the sick. And if we are completely honest, we must admit that we all are sick. Praise God! Because that means Jesus came for us.

We are called to imitate the mission of Jesus. We must extend mercy to everyone, including ourselves. We must reach out to the poor, not only with money, but also with our time and our love. We must treat them with respect. We must give sight to those blind to the truth by lovingly sharing the fullness of faith found in Christ. We must forgive those held in bondage to us by their past wrongs. We must also reach out to accept the freedom from our own bondage, whether we are bound by sin, despair, addiction, egotism, materialism, or something else.

Be merciful as your heavenly father is merciful (cf. Lk 6:36). This statement is a development of a commandment found in the Old Testament Book of Leviticus: "Be holy, for I, the LORD your God, am holy" (Lv 19:2). Though related, what Jesus said was something quite different from Leviticus.

The Levitical command was conveyed by Moses to God's people. For his people, the concept of holiness was steeped strongly in a call to be set apart, since they had been called to avoid the pagan nations and their practices. As previously discussed, when the people failed to heed this call and intermingled with other cultures, they soon gave up their worship of the Lord.

Approximately 1,400 years after Moses revealed this command, Jesus addressed a people with the same conviction. They still believed they were supposed to avoid unnecessary dealings with the Romans, Greeks, Samaritans, and the other peoples around them. It was still commonly thought that illness and misfortune were a sign that the person or the person's ancestors were guilty of sin, so the concept of holiness connoted a need to be set apart from these people as well.

It was to a people who equated holiness with the avoidance of perceived sinners that Jesus proclaimed his message that holiness really means showing mercy to all. Lest there be any question of this interpretation, let us look at what Jesus says immediately before he commanded the people to be merciful: "Love your enemies and do good to them … then your reward will be great and you will be children of the Most High, for he himself is kind to the ungrateful and the wicked" (Lk 6:35).

Who did the people at the time of Jesus hate most? The pagan Roman oppressors. Jesus stood before a crowd of people who felt it was their duty to hate and avoid the Romans. He encouraged these people to show mercy toward the Romans. Jesus also told them that it was more God-like to love the Romans than to love God's Chosen People, saying, "For if you love those who love you, what credit is that to you? Even sinners love those who love them. And if you do good to those who do good to you, what credit is that to you? Even sinners do the same" (Lk 6:32–33).

Jesus tells us all to be merciful as God is merciful. As we seek God's mercy, we must be God's mercy to all whom we encounter—the poor, the lame, the blind, the sinner, and even our enemy.

Forgive seventy-seven times. The amount of mercy that God wishes to be given to all is explained by Jesus in answer to a question by St. Peter.

> Then Peter approaching asked him, "Lord, if my brother sins against me, how often must I forgive him? As many as seven times?" Jesus answered, "I say to you, not seven times but seventy-seven times." (Mt 19:21–22).

If taken literally, this statement means that we are to forgive someone seventy-seven times. Yet Jesus reveals that the mercy of God is even more magnanimous than that. Forgiving someone who has wronged us seventy-seven times seems almost impossible until we honestly look at our lives. Have we not wronged countless people, including our parents, children, spouses, and others? And how many more times than seventy-seven times have we wronged them? Have they not also wronged us more than seventy-seven times? Is God asking us to stop at seventy-seven times, and from then on hold everything against them? Of course not.

What about our sins against God? Is not every sin truly a sin against God? Because of this, over the course of our lives, we have sinned far more than seventy-seven times. Will God refuse to forgive our seventy-eighth sin? Absolutely not.

In Scripture, seven is a number that signifies completeness and perfection. St. Peter was not being ungenerous when he asked Jesus whether he should forgive seven times; instead, he was trying to be a good, righteous person. St. Peter was asking whether forgiveness should be granted in a good, appropriate, and complete amount.

But Jesus answered, "Not seven times, but seventy-seven times." (Sometimes seventy-seven times is translated seventy times seven.) Jesus answered that mercy is not to be granted in a good, appropriate amount. Mercy is not even to be granted overwhelmingly. Rather, mercy is to be granted without limit.

Jesus assures us that there is no end to God's mercy. We will be forgiven seven times seventy-seven times, or even seventy to the seventieth power times. There is no sin that God is not willing to forgive. And God wills that his mercy be poured out through each of us to others. In his response to St. Peter, Jesus speaks to each one of us, "As my heavenly Father is so generous with his mercy toward you, you must likewise be merciful to others."

I desire mercy, not sacrifice. The Gospel of Matthew signifies the great importance of this statement of Jesus by quoting it twice in close proximity (cf. Mt 9:13, 12:7). In both instances, righteous people were looking to find fault in Jesus's actions. In the first instance, Jesus was chastised for eating with tax collectors and other sinners. In the second instance, Jesus was accused of condoning the profanation of the Sabbath by allowing his disciples to pluck ears of grain to eat.

We might find both of these accusations to be foolish, but that's only because we don't fully understand the religious culture in which they occurred. The Jewish people of Jesus's time believed that it was a great sin to eat with notorious sinners, especially tax collectors who were collaborators with the Roman oppressors and who became wealthy by over-charging the people. To associate with such sinners meant that you condoned their actions. To eat with them would result in taking on their defilement. The rules concerning the Sabbath were very legalistic. The prescription for a day of rest had become interpreted to prohibit any kind of work, even something as mundane as picking a head of grain and eating it.

The people who chastised Jesus sought to please God through sacrifice—both the literal sacrifice of animals in the Temple and the figurative sacrifice of one's life to pedantic observance of the letter of the Law. These people, however, did not stop at a personal observance of the Law, but sought to impose sacrifices upon others. Jesus taught against this interpretation of the Law, proclaiming that to show mercy to another is far more pleasing to God than any amount of sacrifice.

We have every reason to believe that the people with whom Jesus dined were in fact grave sinners. The tax collectors had undoubtedly betrayed their fellow Jews through extortion. Accordingly these were exactly the people with whom Jesus would dine. These were the people to whom Jesus would reach out in love. These were the people who needed redemption. These were the people who needed to be welcomed, not shunned.

Jesus turned his critics' understanding of sacrifice upside-down. He taught that true sacrifice involves reaching out in love to another, even when that person is odious to us. True sacrifice involves attending to the sinner without condoning his sin while seeking his repentance. Such a sacrifice is not merely a merciful act but also an act of worship, because the sinner is God's beloved child. What greater offering could possibly be brought before the altar of our Lord than the soul of a repentant sinner?

In promoting mercy over other forms of sacrifice, Jesus teaches us that we cannot earn Heaven. Heaven will not be obtained by keeping score of how many sacrifices we make and how many prayers we say. Objectively, it is a good practice to give up candy or say extra prayers during Lent. But, if we are merely doing these out of a sense of obligation and at the same time refuse to forgive an estranged family member who has wronged us or we gossip about those around us who live an inappropriate lifestyle, we fall short of Jesus's example. We could worship God in a better way. Mercy shown toward these people is the worship Jesus desires of us.

The people that accused Jesus were also hypocritical. Jesus defended his disciples' picking heads of grain by pointing out that David, the hero of the Jews, in his greatest need took the "bread of the Presence" (bread offered on the altar and forbidden to be eaten by anyone but priests) and gave it to his soldiers to eat. Jesus also pointed out that the priests of his time performed many tasks on the Sabbath that could easily be interpreted as work, and therefore prohibited on the Sabbath.

Jesus set things in the right order. He explained that it was more important for David and his followers to eat than to die from starvation while fleeing from the wrath of King Saul. And Jesus explained how it was more important for the priests of his time to perform the ritual worship of God than to avoid all work and thereby neglect their duty. Therefore, it made sense that the disciples should keep up their strength with the heads of grain in order to follow Jesus.

Jesus's message applies as much to us as it did to the people who challenged him. We continually fall into hypocrisy. We constantly complain about laws, rules, and regulations when they apply to us, yet we are the first to condemn our brothers, sisters, spouses, co-workers, or celebrities when they stumble. We show up at Mass and throw a few dollars in the collection plate but ignore a beggar on the street.

Sacrifice and formal worship are meant to bring us closer to God. They help us to recognize God's glory, to praise God, and to thank him for all he has given us. But if either is merely a ritualistic act, distanced from the heart, it is useless. In a way, the greatest act of worship is to call upon God for his mercy. We praise God when we humbly acknowledge that God is God and we are not; that God created everything and gave us everything, including our lives; and that we constantly fail and are undeserving of God's love. We beautifully worship God when we cry out, "Lord, I am not worthy that you should enter under my roof, but only say the word and my soul shall be healed!"

Just like the people in the time of Jesus, we would like to obtain God's good graces through our righteousness. "I followed the commandments." "I kept the Sabbath holy." "I followed all of the rules and regulations." "I said my prayers." "I have merited God's favor." These claims are foolish! The truth is that we all are sinners born into a sinful world. No matter how hard we try, we fail. We sin. We turn from God.

There is no way to "earn our way" into Heaven. When we stand before the gates of Heaven, tens of thousands of rosaries, thousands of days of fasting, and even every Sunday's Mass attendance will not, by themselves, gain us admittance. Our religious observance, done with an attitude of love, will be acknowledged by God. But, we will still be asked if we were merciful toward others.

> When the Son of Man comes in his glory,… He will place the sheep on his right and the goats on his left. Then the king will say to those on his right, "Come, you who are blessed by my Father. Inherit the kingdom prepared for you from the foundation of the world. For I was hungry and you gave me food, I was thirsty and you gave me drink, a stranger and you welcomed me, naked and

you clothed me, ill and you cared for me, in prison and you visited me." ... Amen, I say to you, whatever you did for one of these least brothers of mine, you did for me." (Mt 25:31–40)

Parables of Mercy

Although there is not enough time to discuss all that the parables teach us about the mercy of God, we can benefit greatly from reflecting upon three of the most instructive parables.

The Prodigal Son (cf. Lk 15:11–32). The father in this parable had two sons. The younger was rebellious and the elder dutiful. The younger son demanded his share of the inheritance and left for a foreign land where he squandered it in "loose living." When he hit rock bottom, he returned to his father and asked for his forgiveness (kind of). And the father welcomed him back enthusiastically.

We must be careful not to become so used to this story that it fails to amaze us. The younger son treated his father with utter contempt. By demanding his inheritance, the son effectively was saying his father was already dead to him. He wanted nothing to do with his father. He wanted no relationship with him. He took the money and left. He left not only his father's house, but also his people and homeland. Once completely separated from any relationship with his father, he squandered everything.

It might be a beneficial exercise to adapt this parable to our current day and age. Imagine a son taking a significant portion of his father's home equity, pension, savings, and anything his father owned. Imagine him disowning his father and the rest of the family, flying to Las Vegas to squander everything on drugs, alcohol, prostitutes, and gambling, and then having the audacity to come back to his father and ask him for help.

Before we address the mercy of the father, let us recognize one more thing of import. True heartfelt contrition does not appear to be the younger son's primary motivation for returning home. Rather, the son was spurred into action by the fact that he was broke and homeless and had to feed pigs in order to survive. In fact, the son was so hungry that he was envious of the pig's food. (This is even more notable when we remember that contact with pigs was prohibited by the faith of his people.) Fearing that he would starve to death and recognizing that his father's hired hands were better off than himself, the son practiced a good "I'm sorry" speech and headed back to his father's house.

After making sure that his audience would recognize what a selfish, contemptible sinner the son was, Jesus revealed an ending to the story that was unthinkable. "The father saw him at a distance." The father was waiting for the son, staring out across the fields to catch a glimpse of him, praying every day that the very son who disrespected and disowned him would return. "The father ran to his son." The son had left the father, so it should have been the son who ran back to him. But the son did not come running back, he sheepishly returned with a fairly lame apology. "The father embraced and kissed him." This son was broke, homeless, and had tended pigs. He was ragged and he stunk. But his father ignored the smell of pigs and the odor of betrayal, threw his arms around his beloved son, and showered kisses upon him. "Dress my son with the best robe and put a ring on his finger; prepare the finest meal and let us celebrate, for my son was lost and now is found; he was dead and now is alive." This son asked merely to be given a job and to be fed like a servant; instead, the father washed off his filth, clothed him with the symbols of sonship, and celebrated his return with the fatted calf.

We are the prodigal sons. We continually and purposefully separate ourselves from our heavenly Father. We ignore his commandments. We give in to the temptations of the world. We fail to be grateful for all our blessings. Maybe we give in to the urges of impurity, intoxication, or gossip. Maybe we don't pray as much as we should. Maybe we have stopped going to Mass, or maybe we go to Mass but our hearts are far from God. Maybe we have lied or cheated in dealings with others. Maybe we have committed adultery. Maybe we have had an abortion. Regardless of what we have done, God desires to forgive us. We can choose to run away from God, but he will never run away from us. He waits for us and longs for our return. And when we make even the slightest movement back toward him, our merciful Lord runs to us. He embraces us. He washes us of every stain of sin. Our Lord clothes us in forgiveness and righteousness. And he welcomes us back into his family to live forever with him at the banquet he has prepared for us in Heaven.

The Good Samaritan (cf. Lk 10:25–37). Prior to telling this story, Jesus was confronted by a lawyer (an expert in the law of God). Having identified that the law requires loving God and loving neighbor, the lawyer sought a loophole and asked Jesus who is one's "neighbor." In response, Jesus told him the parable of the good samaritan.

In summary, this parable is the story of a Jewish man who was beaten by robbers and left for dead. A priest and a Levite both passed by the man, but did not help him. A Samaritan, however, took great efforts to care for the Jew. Jesus asked the lawyer who of the three was a "neighbor" to the man in need. The lawyer responded, "The one who showed mercy to him." And Jesus instructed him to "go and do likewise."

This parable is simple but poignant. We can surmise that since the man attacked by bandits was returning from Jerusalem, he was perhaps a good man who had just finished worshiping at the Temple. Regardless, his own people, the priest and Levite, would not help him. Presumably, the priest and Levite refused to help the man because they were on their way to worship at the Temple and to touch the bleeding man would have rendered them ritually impure and, therefore, unable to engage in Temple worship.

It fell upon a Samaritan to help the man. The Samaritans were descendants of original Jewish tribes who had intermingled with other cultures and wandered from the traditional practice of the faith. They were hated by the Jews, and no righteous Jew would have any contact with them. It is taken for granted in the story that any Jew would be justified in not helping a Samaritan in need, regardless of the circumstances.

By this parable, Jesus makes it clear that we do not show love for God by self-righteous, legalistic practices. Instead, we show love for God by being merciful to our neighbor. And the true answer to the lawyer's question, "Who is my neighbor?" is that everyone is your neighbor. Our neighbor is our brother, our friend, our co-worker, and even our "enemy."

What Jesus means by "go and do likewise " is that the lawyer (and we) should endeavor to extend mercy to others as Jesus will always extend it to us. Despite the scandal his teachings caused the "righteous" Jews about him, Jesus always reached out with mercy to those who seemingly deserved none—the tax collectors, adulterers, Samaritans, Roman soldiers—and to anyone and everyone who needed mercy.

If we are honest with ourselves, we must admit that we are the priest and the Levite. We have judged so many people. Maybe we have great contempt for a politician who voted to liberalize abortion laws or a pop artist who uses pornographic lyrics. But these are precisely the "neighbors" who need our love and who need healing. We must also recognize that we are the man bleeding in the road. We find ourselves lying in the gutter of sin and despair. We need forgiveness. We need mercy.

The Pharisee and the Tax Collector (cf. Lk 18:9–14). In this parable, Jesus contrasted two men. One was a Pharisee, a class of people admired by his audience as zealous followers of the law. The other was a tax collector, a member of a class of people vilified by Jesus's audience. The Pharisee stood up boldly in the front of Temple and prayed to God, bragging how great he was and pointing out the tax collector's wretchedness. The tax collector hid in the back, averted his eyes, and beat his breast praying, "God, be merciful to me a sinner!" After contrasting these two, Jesus proclaimed, "I tell you, the latter went home justified, not the former."

There is no need to dwell on the arrogance of the Pharisee; instead, let us focus on the tax collector. The obvious lesson of this story is the beauty of humility. The tax collector recognized that he was a sinner. He recognized that he deserved nothing from God. He bowed low before the majesty of God and simply begged for mercy. But as beautiful as his humility was, we must not forget that the tax collector not only asked for mercy, he received it!

The people to whom Jesus spoke were sure that the sins of the tax collector were unforgivable. He was a damnable sinner whom God disdained. But Jesus was sure of the opposite. This tax collector was a beautiful, beloved child of the Father, regardless of his sins. The Lord did not wish condemnation but complete forgiveness at his repentance. In the tax collector's remorse, his sins were completely forgiven, and he was justified fully in the eyes of his heavenly Father.

God grants mercy to all who ask. There is no sin that we have committed that our Lord is unwilling to forgive. None of us are beyond salvation. Our heavenly Father patiently waits for us to acknowledge our sins and ask for forgiveness. Once we do, he will pour out his infinite mercy upon us so that we will be made new and glorious!

> Though your sins be like scarlet, they may become white as snow;
> Though they be red like crimson, they may become white as wool.
> (Is 1:18)

Jesus's Merciful Passion and Death

The experience of Jesus's Passion and Death. The first mercy of Jesus's Passion and Death is his experience. Jesus, the Son, the second Person of the Blessed Trinity, cast off his glory to embrace excruciating suffering and a gruesome death for our salvation.

Jesus's Passion began in the Garden of Gethsemane. Here Jesus experienced such distress that he exclaimed, "My soul is very sorrowful, even to death" (Mt 26:38). Saints and mystics suggest that in order to expiate our sins, it was necessary for Jesus to experience all of the pain caused by all the sins of humanity. Therefore, in the Garden of Gethsemane, Jesus experienced every temptation imaginable, witnessed every sin that had been or would be committed, and experienced all the pain that had and would result from these sins. In agony, Jesus "prayed more earnestly; and his sweat became like great drops of blood falling down upon the ground" (Lk 22:44).

Jesus was arrested, bound, and dragged off to the high priest's house for trial. He was falsely accused, insulted, spit on, and beaten. Then he was brought before Pontius Pilate, who condemned him to be scourged and crucified.

Prior to the making of the movie *The Passion of the Christ*, many people had very little understanding of the brutality of a Roman scourging. The whips were made of several leather straps to which were attached iron balls and sharp pieces of sheep bones. The iron balls would cause deep contusions, and the bones would tear into the skin and tissue below. As the flogging continued, the whip would "tear into the underlying skeletal muscle and produce quivering ribbons of bleeding flesh."[4]

After his scourging, a crown of thorns was pushed into his skull. Jesus was then made to carry his Cross from the Roman praetorium to a place outside the city called Golgotha. Without

---

[4] "On the Physical Death of Jesus Christ," *Journal of the American Medical Association*, March 1986, p. 1457.

sleep or respite, tortured brutally, and suffering from extreme loss of blood, Jesus was so fatigued and drained that tradition holds he fell three times under the weight of the Cross.

At Golgotha, Jesus's hands and feet were nailed to the Cross. And on the Cross, he continued to suffer taunts and insults. The horror of crucifixion is that it makes it impossible to breathe without pushing up on the feet pierced with nails, flexing the elbows (causing rotation on the nail pierced wrists), while continually rubbing the back (shredded from the scourging) against the rough wood of the cross.[5]

The fullness of the Father's mercy was shown to us when he denied mercy to his own Son, Jesus Christ. The Father allowed Jesus to experience denial, abandonment, scourging, crucifixion, and death, though he deserved none of it. Yet the Father does everything, except remove our free will, to save us sinners from the punishments we fully deserve. This is the mercy of God.

Jesus was sinless. He was falsely accused, and, although he responded in truth, he was convicted anyway. Jesus taught and modeled mercy throughout his life. Yet none was shown to him. Jesus forgave those steeped in sin, though sinless himself, yet he was condemned. Jesus healed the sick, yet was beaten and scourged. Jesus brought the dead back to life, yet was murdered. And let us not exculpate ourselves as we continually fail to show mercy after having already seen the mercy of Jesus. But we must not despair. Jesus knew of our weakness; yet he underwent his Passion and Death for each

---

[5] Ibid, p. 1461.

one of us personally. Despite all our sins and failings, despite our unwillingness to show mercy to our neighbor, and despite our regular rejection of God, Jesus suffered and died for us. And from Jesus's Death and Resurrection, an unending flow of mercy poured out to heal all of our betrayals, to atone for all of our sins, and to make amends for any lack of mercy on our part.

As Jesus hung dying upon the Cross, every thought of his was of mercy for us. Despite the pain it would cause, Jesus called out messages of mercy from the Cross. First, Jesus prayed "Father, forgive them, they know not what they do" (Lk 23:34). Second, he consoled the repentant thief who hung on the Cross next to him, saying, "Amen, I say to you, today you will be with me in Paradise" (Lk 23:43). Third, he entrusted all of us to the tender care of his Blessed Mother, saying to Mary and St. John, "Woman, behold, your son. ... Behold, your mother" (Jn 19:26–27).

The effect of Jesus's Passion and Death. The second mercy of Jesus's Passion and Death is its effect. Jesus took upon himself every sin committed by every human being from the beginning of time until the end of the world. Through the sin of Adam and Eve and through each of our own personal sins, we have offended God and separated ourselves from life in him. Jesus emptied himself of his glory and took the form of a slave in order to endure the punishment we deserved, to pay the price for our sins, and to mend the relationship we rent.

Jesus stated, "No one has greater love than this, to lay down one's life for one's friends" (Jn 15:13). To lay down one's life for an enemy seems almost unfathomable. Yet Jesus did this and more. Jesus laid down his life for those who took it from him. He laid down his life for every person who sinned against him, from the creation of Adam to end of the world. He died for the Jews who condemned him, the Roman guards who flogged him, the crowds who mocked him and spat upon him, and the criminals who died alongside him. He died for each one of us.

In order to heal man, God became man. In order to atone for the sin of man, God offered himself as a sacrifice. Through the pride and disobedience of the man Adam, sin entered the world and death reigned. Through the humble obedience of the man Jesus Christ, sinlessness reentered the world and eternal life was restored.

The effect of Jesus's Passion and Death is that the gates of Heaven are open to each of us. Through the salvific work of Christ, we have been adopted fully as children of God. We are invited to share divine life with God. Our destiny is not the grave, but eternal peace and joy in Heaven.

The Mercy of the Resurrection

The mercy of Jesus's Passion finds its necessary fulfillment in the Resurrection. Without the Resurrection, there would be no meaning to Jesus's Passion and Death. Jesus would have sacrificed himself and died for no purpose. As St. Paul points out in writing to the Corinthians, "If Christ has not been raised, then empty is our preaching; empty, too, your faith" (1 Cor 15:14).

Many people have sacrificed their lives nobly throughout history. All of the Apostles except St. John were martyred for spreading the Gospel message. Today in much of the world, men and women continue to be martyred for their faith in Jesus. If there is no resurrection of the body and death is the end, then the Apostles and martyrs are fools. If this short mortal life is all that we possess, to throw it away one second earlier than we must is utter stupidity.

Christ's Resurrection imparts meaning to every aspect of our lives. Our greatest sorrows are bearable because of the great joy that awaits us. The fear of death is tempered by the hope of the afterlife. Our trials and tribulations can be prayerfully joined to the sufferings of Christ, so as to make them useful for our own spiritual good and the good of others.

In his first letter, St. Peter exalts, "Blessed be the God and Father of our Lord Jesus Christ, who in his great mercy gave us a new birth to a living hope through the Resurrection of Jesus Christ from the dead, to an inheritance that is imperishable, undefiled, and unfading" (1 Pt 1:3–4). In rising from the dead, Jesus did not merely promise, but showed us our inheritance. Through his example, Jesus revealed the resurrection that awaits us.

The Resurrection is the sure and sufficient hope given to us by our merciful God. No other person has died and then risen from the dead never to die again. No religious leader before or after Christ has conquered death.

In God's mercy, Jesus did not die with the final words, "Trust me, I am going to Heaven, and you will meet me when you die." God is too merciful for that. He knows that this would not have provided enough hope for us. So Jesus died and rose from the dead. He revealed himself fully alive, not only to his close followers but to hundreds of others as well. Jesus walked with them, spoke with them, ate with them, and even invited one in particular, St. Thomas, to touch the holes in his hands and side so that there would be no doubts.

It is a fact that Jesus rose from the dead. If he did not rise from the dead, all of his teachings would be proven false and he would be a failure. If Jesus did not rise from the dead, then he could not be God. And, if not God, then Jesus was either a liar or a lunatic. The very Gospels that attest to the Resurrection admit this with almost no exception. Jesus's followers abandoned him at his Death. The only thing that changed their minds was his Resurrection. All of the Apostles (except St. John) and countless other disciples died rather than renounce their belief that Jesus was God. Did they do this out of loyalty to a liar or lunatic? No! They died for their risen Lord!

In his great mercy, God revealed what he has in store for us. We are not made to die but to live forever. We, like Jesus, will have bodies neither subject to pain or death nor constrained by time or space, but glorified and capable of perfect union with all creation and our Creator.

We remain subject to the stain of sin, but we are destined for glory. In God's mercy, he gave us, through the Resurrection of Jesus, a taste of what is to come. The Resurrection sustains us as we suffer the trials of this world. The Resurrection points us toward our final destination. The Resurrection reveals the merciful glory God has in store for us.

FOUR

The Apostolic Movement of Divine Mercy

Background

As we have seen, God's mercy is prevalent throughout the Old Testament and finds its perfection in Jesus. Yet, in our weakness, we still struggle to recognize and embrace the mercy of God. It is for this reason that God reached out to a simple Polish nun, Sister Maria Faustina Kowalska, in the 1920s in order to facilitate a tremendous leap forward in our understanding of God's mercy.

Born in 1905, Helen Kowalska felt called to enter the convent when she was in her late teens. Assessing Helen for possible acceptance into the Congregation of the Sisters of our Lady of Mercy, the superior of the convent described her as "no one special."[1] But it is with this "no one special" that our Lord chose to enter into a unique and intimate relationship that has only been experienced by a handful of saints. It is to this "no one special" that God revealed with new clarity the depths of his mercy and the practical means for embracing his mercy. It is

---

[1] Maria Faustina Kowalska, *Diary: Divine Mercy in My Soul* (Stockbridge, MA: Marians of the Immaculate Conception, 2002), p. xxix.

this "no one special" who articulated God's mercy with wisdom beyond that of any theologian who preceded her: "Out of the mouths of infants and nurslings you have brought forth praise" (Mt 21:16).

In the short thirteen years she spent in the convent before her death, St. Faustina received mystical experiences in which Jesus appeared to her and revealed a special message of mercy for the whole world. It is important to understand that this was not a new revelation by God, but a re-revealing of the message contained in Scripture and personified by the life of Christ. Practically speaking, it was if we had been staring at a masterpiece in a dimly lit room and suddenly spotlights were tuned on. Or as if we had been listening to a beautiful orchestra and finally realized we had been wearing earplugs.

God revealed his great mercy not only through the words he spoke to St. Faustina but also through the life she lived. It was to one who was merciful that God revealed his mercy. It was to one who was completely humble that God revealed his greatness.

In the wake of these revelations, the publication of St. Faustina's personal diary, and her canonization, the Church has seen what can only be referred to as a bold movement of the Holy Spirit. This "Apostolic Movement of Divine Mercy" continues to unfold and gain speed. In the next few sections of this book we will only touch upon the depths of the message of mercy revealed by God to St. Faustina. Accordingly, it would be to the reader's great spiritual benefit to explore the movement of Divine Mercy by reading St. Faustina's diary and the many wonderful publications that explain the message and its movement.

I Am Love and Mercy

In St. Faustina's lengthy diary, there is one statement by our Lord that encapsulates the entire message of mercy: "I am Love and Mercy itself" (*Diary*, 1047). God's very nature is love. God's very nature is mercy. God does not merely exhibit love. God *is* love. God doesn't merely act mercifully, but *is* mercy itself.

The importance of this distinction cannot be overstated. Each of us acts lovingly at times, and at others, not so much. Each of us has the capacity to show mercy toward others, yet often acts unmercifully. To merely exhibit an attribute such as love or mercy allows for the possibility that the attribute might not always be forthcoming. But if love and mercy are not merely attributes, but identities, the possibility of cessation of love and mercy is impossible.

Our Triune God is infinite and unchanging. There was never a time that God was not love and mercy. There will never be a time when God will not be love and mercy. Before any of us ever rejected God or sinned in any way, our Lord was prepared to forgive us. After any sin, God offers complete forgiveness. Upon any effort on our part to isolate ourselves from God, he reaches out to invite us back. Like the father in the parable of the prodigal son, Our Lord has his gaze always set on us. He waits patiently for us to approach him. Upon our mildest, meekest, most unworthy request for his mercy, our Father embraces us in his merciful arms and engulfs us in the robe of his tender love.

Our Lord revealed to St. Faustina more clearly the incredible depth of his mercy. His mercy is endless. And his mercy is for all, without exception. Through his words to St. Faustina, Jesus begged us to ask for his mercy and assured us that he will pour out his mercy upon our every request: "Souls that make an appeal to my mercy delight me. To such souls I grant even more graces than they ask" (*Diary*, 1146). There is no unforgivable sin, except the sin of failing to desire forgiveness. There is no one whom Jesus is unwilling to forgive. Rather, the greater the sinner, the more Jesus wishes to be merciful: "[Let] the greatest sinners place their trust in my mercy...I cannot punish even the greatest sinner if he makes an appeal to my compassion" (*Diary*, 1146).

Throughout history God revealed his desire to show mercy. He spoke through the patriarchs, judges, kings, and prophets, constantly assuring his people of his forgiveness and mercy. Then our God became incarnate and personally assured us that he would always grant us mercy if we asked, especially to those most in need. Yet we continue to doubt the mercy of our God. We look at the evil in the world and in our own hearts, and cannot fathom how good can come from such evil. We cannot fathom a God who could love us so much as to forgive such wretchedness.

In response to these doubts of ours, our Lord has assured us again through his words to St. Faustina. Not only does our Lord offer mercy to all, he offers it first and foremost to the soul least deserving of mercy. God offers the greatest healing to the one who is most ill. He offers the greatest forgiveness to the one most at fault. God offers the greatest hope to the one most in despair:

When a soul sees and realizes the gravity of its sins, when the whole abyss of misery into which it has immersed itself is displayed before its eyes, let it not despair, but with trust let it throw itself into the arms of my mercy, as a child into the arms of its beloved mother. These souls have right of priority to my compassionate Heart, they have first access to my mercy. (*Diary*, 1541)

Image of Mercy

Recognizing the ability of an image to move our hearts when words fail, Our Lord commanded St. Faustina to have the Image of Divine Mercy painted. The Image, which he set into the imagination of St. Faustina, depicted Jesus looking directly at the viewer. His right hand was raised in a gesture of blessing. His left hand gently touched his breast, from which rays of red and white emanated.

Our Lord explained that the rays represent blood and water. The pale ray is the "Water which makes souls righteous. The red ray stands for the Blood which is the life of souls" (*Diary*, 299). The Image reminds all of us of the mercy won for us by our Lord on the Cross. As Jesus had consummated the sacrifice of himself and hung dead upon the Cross, a soldier pierced his side with a spear, and blood and water flowed out (cf. Jn 19:34).

The mercy of God flows from Jesus. The water that flowed from Jesus's side is the water of Baptism that cleanses us of our sins and welcomes us into God's family. The blood that flowed from Jesus on the Cross is the price for the redemption offered by the Sacrament of Reconciliation, and it is the divine life imparted through the Holy Eucharist. We are made clean by the purity of Jesus. We are washed in the blood of the Lamb. We receive the very life of Jesus when we eat his Body and drink his Blood.

This Image of Divine Mercy is completed with the words given to St. Faustina and inscribed on the Image itself: "Jesus, I trust in You" (*Diary*, 47). These words are a fitting response to the mercy of God, and they also become the prayer invoked in the heart of one who views the Image of Mercy. "Jesus, I trust in you!" has become the constant mantra of hope in God's infinite mercy, and this mantra invokes many other thoughts within our heart: I trust in your mercy. I trust that you can and will forgive me for all of my sins. I trust that you have a plan for me. I trust that you are present even when I have turned away from you. I trust that you are concerned for me even when I cannot feel your presence. I trust that your love for me is infinite. I trust that one day I will be with you, my Lord, in the joy of Heaven.

The Catholic Church is imbued with beautiful things designed to bring souls closer to God. These include the architecture of majestic cathedrals and basilicas, the paintings and sculptures of artists such as Michelangelo, Raphael, and Caravaggio, sacred music such as Gregorian chant, and beautiful vestments and vessels. Two beautiful images that stand out as means for communicating God's mercy are the crucifix and the Image of Divine Mercy.

Throughout the history of the Church, the crucifix has stood as an enduring reminder of God's mercy through Christ's Passion and Death. The crucifix is displayed prominently in churches, found on altars, hung on the walls of homes, and worn around people's necks. The crucifix is formally venerated during the Good Friday liturgy and informally venerated by many of the faithful at the beginning and end of the Rosary.

The Image of Divine Mercy complements the crucifix. It reminds us of God's mercy shown through Christ's Resurrection. In the brief time since the Church has started promoting the Apostolic Movement of Divine Mercy, the Divine Mercy Image has found a prominent place in a great number of churches across the world.

The Image of Divine Mercy is much more than just another beautiful portrayal of Jesus. Our Lord revealed to St. Faustina that the artistry of the Image was not as important as the powerful grace he would bestow through the Image: "Not in the beauty of the color, nor of the brush lies the greatness of this Image, but in My grace" (*Diary*, 313). Jesus revealed to St. Faustina that he desired that the Image be venerated throughout the world, making this depiction of Jesus unlike any other artistic depiction (cf. *Diary*, 47). And Jesus promised that many graces would flow out to the souls who venerate the Image. The Image would be the "vessel" for an outpouring of graces from the fountain of mercy (*Diary*, 327). Jesus also promised that "the soul that will venerate this Image *will not perish*" (*Diary*, 48, emphasis added)!

Hour of Mercy

Three o'clock in the afternoon is the hour at which our Lord expired on the Cross (cf. Mt 27:45; Mk 15:33; Lk 23:44). Jesus revealed to St. Faustina that this hour is to be recognized as the "hour of mercy." Speaking to each of us through St. Faustina, Jesus asks, "If only for a brief moment, immerse yourself in My Passion, particularly in My abandonment at the moment of agony" (*Diary*, 1320). Jesus invites us to intimately share in his Suffering and Death.

We are all invited at three o'clock to turn in prayer to Christ's Passion. We might pray the Stations of the Cross or the Chaplet of Divine Mercy or spend some time before the Blessed Sacrament. These practices are great, yet we might not have time for them during the hour of mercy. Jesus, who is not a taskmaster but a merciful God, is mindful of our daily responsibilities and our weakness in committing significant time to prayer. And so, Jesus merely asks that we "immerse ourselves in prayer" wherever we find ourselves during this hour of mercy, even if only for a "very brief instant" (*Diary*, 1572).

Jesus promises great blessings upon those who prayerfully enter into his Passion at the hour of mercy. Every grace is "for the asking" during the hour, both for ourselves and those for whom we pray (*Diary*, 1572). Jesus assures us, "In this hour, I will refuse nothing to the soul that makes a request of me in virtue of My Passion" (*Diary*, 1320).

In embracing the practice of the hour of mercy, it is important not to view God in a morbid way; he does not require us to prayerfully self-flagellate. Instead, Jesus's invitation to daily enter into his Passion is a gift. He has already suffered for us. He has already died for us. And because of this sacrifice, the gates of Heaven are open to us. Christ does not ask us to bear his Cross or feel his pain as a punishment for sin. Rather, Christ offers us the honor of being his companion at the hour of his triumph.

Can meditating upon the sufferings of Christ bring us to tears? Absolutely. But what wonderful tears they can be! They are tears of sadness for sin. They are tears over the suffering of our Lord. They are also tears of joy because Jesus willingly and lovingly underwent suffering and death so that we might be saved. Because he suffered and died for us, we are saved from everything that separates us from Jesus. We are saved for an eternal life with him. This is neither the "hour of sadness" nor the "hour of suffering." It is the hour of great mercy!

Chaplet of Divine Mercy

Our Lord revealed to St. Faustina a powerful prayer called the "Chaplet of Divine Mercy." Using a rosary, St. Faustina was taught to say on the first three beads an Our Father, a Hail Mary, and the Apostles' Creed. On the following large beads, which typically stand as reminders for reciting the Our Father, St. Faustina was taught to pray: "Eternal Father, I offer You the Body and Blood, Soul and Divinity of Your dearly beloved Son, Our Lord Jesus Christ, in atonement for our sins and those of the whole world." On the small beads, which typically stand as reminders for reciting the Hail Mary, she was taught to pray: "For the sake of His sorrowful Passion, have mercy on us and on the whole world." St. Faustina was instructed to conclude the chaplet by repeating three times the words: "Holy God, Holy Mighty One, Holy

Immortal One, have mercy on us and on the whole world"
(*Diary*, 476).

Not only did Our Lord reveal this prayer to St. Faustina, but
he also revealed his desire that all should fervently embrace
this prayer and assured her of its great efficacy. Jesus promised
that through this prayer he would reveal his "infinite mercy"
and "grant unimaginable graces," stating, "Even if there were
a sinner most hardened, if he were to recite this chaplet only
once, he would receive grace" (*Diary*, 687).

Our Lord spoke to St. Faustina about the particular power
of the chaplet to win eternal salvation for souls. He assured
her that anyone who prays the chaplet will receive great
mercy at their death (*Diary*, 687): "At the hour of their death,
I defend as My own glory every soul that will say this chaplet"
(*Diary*, 811). Our Lord also assured St. Faustina that each of us
can help others obtain great mercy by praying the chaplet for
them. Further, our Lord revealed a beautiful image of mercy
gained at the hour of death through praying the chaplet for
the dying: "When they say this chaplet in the presence of the
dying, I will stand between My Father and the dying person,
not as the just Judge, but as the merciful Savior" (*Diary*, 1541).

At first, these claims regarding the power of the chaplet
may seem fantastic. Perhaps praying the chaplet for a dying
sinner seems to resemble a desperate attempt to play a get-
out-of-jail-free card against God. But any doubt over the
truth of these messages is born of our natural inability to
comprehend just how loving and merciful is our God. Our
God does not want us to perish. Our God does not want us to
be separated from him for an instant, let alone eternity.

An accurate but woefully inadequate image of our God would see him cheering us on from the stands as we run a race. A more adequate image would see him convincing the field judge (himself) to let us start again, even after one hundred false starts in a row. If we fell, he would jump out onto the track to help us up. If we gave up and sat down, he would run to our side and beg us to try again, and then he would run next to us and coax us forward. If we felt we had nothing left, he would offer to carry us across the finish line. This is the God who begs us to ask for mercy for ourselves and anyone else. This is the God who unreservedly grants our requests for mercy.

The chaplet isn't a magical formula but a statement of sublime truth and a request of a God who wants nothing more than to grant the request. To better understand why the chaplet is so profound, let us break it down.

Eternal Father. The first two words of the chaplet are a glorious prayer of praise, a statement of faith, and an act of love. We acknowledge that God is both eternal God and our Father. Before we ask anything of God in the chaplet, we first honor him as Eternal God and embrace him as our own Father.

I offer You the Body and Blood, Soul and Divinity of Your dearly beloved Son, Our Lord Jesus Christ. Through these words we make another act of faith and an act of humility. We profess the full divinity and full humanity of Jesus. We acknowledge the truth that it is only through Christ's Body and Blood that we are saved (cf. Jn 6:48–57). We acknowledge Jesus as our *Lord*, our master, that is, the one who has legitimate authority over us and deserves our obedience. We also recognize that it is Jesus who has won our salvation through the Passion of his Body and the spilling of his Blood. And we embrace this perfect offering of Jesus for our sakes as the perfect prayer—by God and to God—on our behalf.

In atonement for our sins and those of the whole world. By these words, we do exactly what God has asked us to do since the beginning of time: we call upon and rely upon his infinite mercy. God continually reaches out to his people and to us individually. He asks us to request his forgiveness for our sins. Regardless of how often we turn away from him, he invites us to return. No matter how grave our sin, God offers complete forgiveness. The Father sent his Son to become man, suffer, and die so that we could obtain the very glory of Heaven. In response, we need only to do one thing to receive this grace—ask for it.

For the sake of His sorrowful Passion, have mercy on us and on the whole world. This simple refrain reiterates our request for mercy and acknowledges how this mercy is won for us. Jesus paid the debt owed to God that mankind could not pay. Jesus sacrificed himself for us so that we might have eternal life. We ask God if we might receive the mercy Jesus won for us through his sacrifice.

Holy God, Holy Mighty One, Holy Immortal One, have mercy on us and on the whole world. By these words we again praise God, acknowledging him as the one, mighty, holy, and immortal God. We bask in God's glory, and we acknowledge his power to grant or deny us mercy, assured that he will grant it to us if we ask. And we show love and mercy to our neighbor by requesting mercy on their behalf as well.

The chaplet is both simple and profound. It is easy to pray, yet more powerful than some long-winded, flowery petition. It is not a get-out-of-jail-free card, but more closely resembles a presidential pardon. God is not forced to grant us mercy because we recite the prayer. Rather, God pours out an ocean of mercy to engulf us because he wants to and because we sincerely ask for mercy. But we must remember that God honors our free will, so we must truly desire his mercy and ask for it.

Feast of Mercy

Our Lord revealed to St. Faustina his desire that the Church embrace Divine Mercy in a special way by celebrating a Feast of Mercy (*Diary*, 49, 965). Jesus requested that on the Sunday following Easter Sunday the Divine Mercy Image be "solemnly blessed" and "venerated publicly" so that all might come to know about it (*Diary*, 341). He promised St. Faustina that, on that day, he would "pour out a whole ocean of graces upon those souls who approach the font of mercy" and "the soul that will go to Confession and receive Holy Communion shall obtain complete forgiveness of sins and punishment" (*Diary*, 699; cf. *Diary*, 1109).

During his homily at the canonization of St. Faustina, St. John Paul II (now canonized himself) established the Feast of Mercy on the Sunday after Easter to be referred to thereafter as Divine Mercy Sunday. On this day, we are encouraged to (1) repent of our sins and go to Confession (this can also be done in the days leading up to or following the Feast), (2) receive Holy Communion, (3) venerate (make an act of great respect before) the Image, (4) be merciful toward others, and (5) trust completely in the God's mercy.

Because our Lord desired to completely forgive sin and punishment through this feast, St. John Paul II granted special indulgences for the remission of the just punishment to which souls would otherwise be subjected. He decreed:

> A plenary indulgence, granted under the usual conditions (sacramental confession, Eucharistic communion and prayer for the intentions of Supreme Pontiff) to the faithful who, on the Second Sunday of Easter or Divine Mercy Sunday, in any church or chapel, in a spirit that is completely detached from the affection for a sin, even a venial sin, take part in the prayers and devotions held in honor of Divine Mercy, or who, in the presence of the Blessed Sacrament exposed or reserved in the tabernacle, recite the Our Father and the Creed, adding a devout prayer to the merciful Lord Jesus (e.g., Merciful Jesus, I trust in you).

> A partial indulgence, granted to the faithful who, at least with a contrite heart, pray to the merciful Lord Jesus a legitimately approved invocation.[2]

For those who cannot go to church or the seriously ill, St. John Paul II decreed:

> Who for a just cause cannot leave their homes or who carry out an activity for the community which cannot be postponed, may obtain a plenary indulgence on Divine Mercy Sunday, if totally detesting any sin, as has been said before, and with the intention of fulfilling as soon as possible the three usual conditions, will recite the Our Father and the Creed before a devout image of Our Merciful Lord Jesus and, in addition, pray a devout invocation to

---

[2] Apostolic Penitentiary, *Decree on Indulgences attached to devotions in honor of Divine Mercy* (June 29, 2002).

the Merciful Lord Jesus (e.g., Merciful Jesus, I trust in you). If it is impossible that people do even this, on the same day they may obtain the Plenary Indulgence if with a spiritual intention they are united with those carrying out the prescribed practice for obtaining the Indulgence in the usual way and offer to the Merciful Lord a prayer and the sufferings of their illness and the difficulties of their lives, with the resolution to accomplish as soon as possible the three conditions prescribed to obtain the plenary indulgence.[3]

It is to our great benefit that this Feast of Mercy has been instituted. How fortunate we are to have such a beautiful opportunity to acknowledge and appreciate the mercy of God. How blessed we are that God throws open the floodgates and releases the torrent of mercy in response to our little efforts to love him better on that day.

---

[3] Ibid.

FIVE

Receiving Mercy

Necessity of Receiving Mercy

Before we address the challenge of receiving mercy, it would benefit us to make sure that, five chapters into this book, we are all on the same page. All of us are in great need of mercy. As St. Paul states rather soberly, "There is no one just…no one who understands…no one who seeks God…not one who does good" (Rom 3:10–12).

In using somewhat harsh language, St. Paul states the basic truth that none of us are perfect. In fact, we are far from it. Each of us is a sinner. We have been sinning since we could exercise our free will. We sin against God, against our neighbor, and against ourselves, and we will continue to sin until the day we die.

St. Paul is not, however, seeking to crush our spirits. Rather, he identifies our sin in order to stress the necessity of God's mercy. This apparent condemnation by St. Paul is resolved by his assurance that while "all have sinned and are deprived of the glory of God," all too "are justified…through the redemption in Christ Jesus" (Rom 3:23–24).

St. Paul points out both the reality of sin and the assurance of hope. He spurs us into recognizing our sin in order to recognize our need for mercy. St. Paul highlights the illness and then prescribes the cure. We are sick in sin and will be healed perfectly through mercy.

No good comes from overemphasizing our guilt. The goal of our self-condemnation is not to wallow in shame, but to recognize our need for healing. We have all been created "very good" by our loving Father. All of us have the capacity to come to know God. All of us have the basic inclination to love. But all of us fall woefully short of perfection. Each of us sins against God, our neighbors, and ourselves. Each of us is in great need of mercy from God, our neighbors, and ourselves.

Difficulty of Receiving Mercy

Pride is the greatest obstacle to mercy. In order for us to receive mercy, we must swallow our pride and admit that it is our fault: We must admit that we have broken God's commands. We must admit that we have willfully rejected God's love. We must admit that we have chosen to separate ourselves from a healthy relationship with God. And we must also admit that we have wronged our neighbors and that we have inflicted harm upon ourselves. Through our deliberate words and actions and our selfish inattentiveness, we have wounded many people, especially those we love most. We also continually make bad choices that result in our detriment.

Failure is just the first thing we must humbly accept. We must also acknowledge that we are weak, and that many wrongful acts against God, our neighbors, and ourselves, arise because we are weak. We are not perfect. We cannot be perfect. No matter how great our desires or efforts, we will always fall short of perfection.

The humility necessary to receive mercy is not fully achieved by acknowledging our sins. We must also acknowledge the innumerable blessings that we receive every day through no merit of our own. We do not deserve our lives, the air we breathe, our keen intellects, or the beauty of a sunrise. Nor does anyone owe us a helpful hand, a kind word, or a smile. Our existence is a gift from God. The love of parents, spouses, siblings, or friends is their gift to us. Even our own accomplishments are inseparable from the natural gifts we have been given and the actions of others around us that led to the occasion of our success.

Mercy might pervade our lives, but we must humbly admit that we don't deserve it; it is impossible to deserve mercy or earn it. By definition, mercy is freely given. Anything that is earned is obtained through justice, not mercy. In the parable of the laborers in the vineyard, the landowner went out four times throughout the day to hire day laborers to work in his vineyard. At the end of the day, the landowner paid each of the workers the normal wage for a full day's work (cf. Mt 20:1–16). The wages given to the first set of workers were just. The same wages given to those who worked only a fraction of the day were merciful.

Mercy is something given to someone who has earned nothing. The reception of mercy involves a complete lack of control. While we should both desire and ask for mercy, we can't obtain it through our own actions. All we can do is humbly request it and then accept it when it is freely given.

It can be difficult to receive mercy from God. We must admit that God is God and we are not. God is Creator and we are creatures. When we receive mercy from God, we must recognize that every atom of the physical world and every non-corporeal element of our experience (e.g., our thoughts and emotions, the concept of time, our sense of "being") are completely dependent upon God for their existence.

We must acknowledge our sins to receive the mercy of God. Despite everything that God gives to us, we constantly ignore and reject him. Mindful of our sins, we must humbly accept God's complete forgiveness. We must also accept all of the blessings he bestows directly and indirectly upon us. This includes accepting his constant gifts even while we are running away from him.

We cannot earn mercy from God, as there is nothing he needs from us. Nor can we repay God for his mercy, as there is nothing we possess that is of equal value. The challenge in accepting fully the mercy of God is to acknowledge it as pure gift. In the passage from the Letter to the Romans that we discussed in the previous section, St. Paul makes this abundantly clear: "Since all have sinned and fall short of the glory of God, they are now justified by his grace *as a gift*, through the redemption that is in Christ Jesus" (Rom 3:23–24, NRSV, emphasis added).

The challenge of accepting God's mercy is also a cause for joy. God loves us so much that he showers mercy upon us though we don't deserve it. St. Paul explains, "For Christ, while we were still helpless, yet died at the appointed time for the ungodly. Indeed, only with difficulty does one die for a just person, though perhaps for a good person one might even find courage to die. But God proves his love for us in that while we were still sinners Christ died for us" (Rom 5:6–8).

Not only is it difficult to receive mercy from God, but it is also difficult to receive mercy from our brothers and sisters. Both require that we admit our faults and our need for someone else. Pride tempts us to avoid asking for mercy or accepting it from another. We fear that if we recognize our need for mercy, we admit our weakness to them and admit that they are better than we are. God does not love some more or less than others, but instead loves everyone equally and wishes that everyone would be merciful and be open to receiving mercy. St. John Paul II pointed out that in giving and receiving mercy, both individuals benefit greatly. The receiver of mercy benefits by the gracious receptivity of merciful love. The giver of mercy also benefits when his mercy is received graciously because it allows him or her to become more Christ-like.[1]

Means for Receiving Mercy

Ask. The first step in receiving mercy is to ask for it. As simple as it sounds, this is a crucial step. Jesus constantly admonishes us to petition God (cf., e.g., Mt 7:7; Lk 11:9; Jn 14:13). His parables teach the power of persistent petition (cf., e.g., Lk 18:1–9, the parable of the persistent widow). Jesus urged people he met everywhere to ask for mercy. In fact, the Gospels abound with stories that attest to the need for and power of asking for mercy. The blind ask Jesus for sight, and

---

[1] John Paul II, *Dives in misericordia*, 14.

they see (cf., e.g., Lk 18:35–43). Cripples ask, and they walk (cf., e.g., Mk 2:1–12). Lepers ask, and they are made clean (cf., e.g., Mt 8:1–3). Tax collectors and adulteresses ask, and their sins are forgiven (cf., e.g., Lk 19:1–8; Jn 8:1–11).

Jesus never forced his mercy upon anyone who did not desire it. There were occasions when Jesus approached someone in need and offered to help, as he did with the sick man near the pool of Bethesda, but even on these occasions that person still had to ask for mercy. This need to ask is highlighted in Jesus's healing of the blind beggar.

There was a blind man begging on the road to Jericho as Jesus passed by, surrounded by a large crowd. Upon learning that Jesus was passing by, the man shouted out, "Jesus, Son of David, have mercy on me!" People in the crowd told him to stop shouting, but the man "shouted out even more loudly, 'Son of David, have mercy on me!'" Jesus stopped and had the man brought to him. Jesus asked him, "What do you want me to do for you?" The man replied "Lord, let me see again." Jesus replied, "Receive your sight; your faith has saved you" (Lk 18:35–43, NRSV).

Jesus could have healed the man after the man's first shout, but Jesus required him to persist in his shouts, despite the criticism of the crowds. Jesus could have just flicked a miracle at the man and kept walking. Instead, he stopped and engaged the man. Jesus made the man ask him for mercy. In response to the man's request, Jesus did not merely remove the man's blindness, but granted spiritual healing as well, declaring that the man's faith had saved him.

Our Lord can anticipate our needs even before we are aware of them. He knows of our hidden desire for mercy. But often that quiet whisper is not enough for us to be healed. Rather, God knows that for our own good we need to humbly ask, cry out, and even beg for mercy. We need to overcome the pride that separates us from God and admit to ourselves that we need his mercy. We need to grow in our faith, and so turn to God, completely trusting in his infinite mercy.

The same need to ask applies to receiving mercy from our neighbor. Unlike God, our neighbor is not omniscient. Despite our belief to the contrary, many times our parents, spouses, siblings, children, or friends do not know that we are sorry or that we need help. Other times they are aware, but their pride or other personal wounds prevent them from reaching out to us with mercy.

We must ask for mercy. If we have wronged our neighbor, we must apologize and ask for forgiveness. If we are "blind," "lame," "poor," or in need of any physical or spiritual assistance, we must reach out and ask for help. Our request for mercy is a great act of humility, respect, and love.

When we request mercy from our neighbor, we humbly recognize that we are not self-sufficient but need help to both survive and thrive. We need the physical, emotional, and spiritual assistance of others. We need their clemency, compassion, and understanding. When we ask for forgiveness, we show respect by admitting our wrongs. When we ask for help, we show respect for another's ability to accomplish that which we cannot. A request of mercy to our neighbor is an act of love. It is a recognition of their worth. It is a gift to them of the ability to be vessels of God's own Divine Mercy.

Accept. The second step in receiving mercy is to accept mercy. This step also sounds simple, but it is absolutely necessary. In fact, refusing to accept mercy is the only unforgivable sin.

God's first gift to us after life was the gift of free will. Because God loves us and wants us to love him in return, he had to give us the ability to choose to receive or reject his love. While God always offers us the gift of mercy, we always have the ability to refuse it.

Jesus declared that all sins could be forgiven except "blasphemy against the Holy Spirit" (Mk 12:31, Mk 3:28–29; Lk 12:10). The Church explains that blasphemy against the Spirit is the refusal to allow the Holy Spirit to work toward the sanctification of a soul; it is the refusal to accept the mercy of God.

The only "unforgivable sin" is that for which a person refuses to be forgiven.[2] At first, the concept of an "unforgivable sin" might seem unjust and unmerciful, but it is neither. It is both just and merciful for God to offer mercy and allow us to reject it. It is not only just and merciful, it is absolutely necessary for us to possess free will.

God's mercy is available even to the last instant of a person's life. The worst sinner of all time could, as he drew his last breath, repent and claim God's mercy and it would be granted to him. This underscores the incredible mercy of God. He wishes to pour out his mercy upon each of us no matter what we have done. But this also underscores the practical reality of our unwillingness to receive God's mercy. At every moment of our lives, God stands ready to forgive us for previous sins

---

[2] John Paul II, *Dominum et vivificantem* (May 18, 1986), no. 46.

and impart his grace. If we refuse this gift of God's mercy for the majority of our lives, what realistic expectation is there that we will, on our deathbed, finally ask for and accept it?

With regards to our neighbors, we must not accept mercy merely for our sake, but for their sake as well. As we have discussed, our receptivity to the mercy of others increases our humility and our ability to love. To receive mercy from another is also an act of love toward the one who offers mercy because it allows him to be merciful.

Move on. The third step in receiving mercy is to presume it has been given and then move on. Forgiveness isn't a feeling. It's a fact. What we feel after we ask God for mercy isn't important. All that matters is that we ask and are willing to receive mercy.

Sometimes when we receive the Sacrament of Reconciliation, we feel truly forgiven. We might feel as if a terrible weight has been lifted off of us. We might also feel great peace. Or we might feel nothing. But it doesn't matter. We *are* forgiven!

In our regular prayer requests for God's mercy and blessings, we might see a pattern where God has answered and is continuing to answer our prayers. Or we might be blind to God's action in our lives. It doesn't matter because God hears us and answers us in a way that will be to our eternal benefit.

As we pray the Chaplet of Divine Mercy at our mother's bedside as she expires, we might feel great peace and feel assured that she is in Heaven. Or we might just feel loss and emptiness at her departure from our lives. Again, it doesn't matter. God has heard our prayer and will keep his promise of mercy.

Sometime we hear deep within us, "You are not good enough; you don't deserve mercy. Since you cannot see or feel

God's mercy, he has not granted it." We must ignore these lies whispered by the voice of doubt and embrace the shouts of truth that emanate from the very mouth of God:

> If you ask anything of me in my name, I will do it. (Jn 14:14)

> Ask and it will be given to you; seek and you will find; knock and the door will be opened to you. For everyone who asks, receives; and the one who seeks, finds; and to the one who knocks, the door will be opened. (Mt 7:7–8)

> Souls that appeal to my mercy delight me. I grant them more graces than they request. I cannot punish even the greatest sinner if he makes an appeal to my compassion. (*Diary*, 1146)

God himself has spoken. He has assured us that, if we ask for mercy, it *will* be granted. And God does not lie. So, taking to heart the words of St. Paul, "Let us confidently approach the throne of grace to receive mercy" (Heb 4:16). God answers our prayers for mercy. Once we have asked for mercy, we must tell ourselves that it has been granted and then move on with our lives.

Sacraments of Mercy

Entire books have been devoted to addressing the mercy that God pours out through the Sacraments. We certainly cannot do them justice in one short section. We would, however, be remiss if we did not at least acknowledge the importance of the Sacraments and how they impart mercy in our lives.

Baptism. It is through Baptism that we are washed of "Original Sin." (Original Sin is that which entered into the world through the sin of Adam and Eve and that which we inherit.) In justice, we are conceived without the ability to obtain eternal joy in Heaven. At conception, we are created in the image and likeness of God, but not in possession of the Divine Life of the Trinity. Baptism cleanses us of Original Sin, and we are radically changed. We are reborn of "water and the Spirit" (Jn 3:5). We are given grace, the very Divine Life of God. We are adopted as children of God and become members of the Body of Christ. We are co-heirs with Christ to the eternal glory of Heaven (cf. *CCC*, 1262–67). Baptism also cleanses us of all the actual (not original) sin we have committed and acquits us of any punishment due therefrom.

Reconciliation. The Sacrament of Reconciliation is often referred to as the "Sacrament of Mercy." In this Sacrament, we come before our Lord and humbly confess our sins, and, in return, Our Lord forgives them. Our Lord empowered priests to act in his stead and gave them his power to forgive any and all sins: "Amen, I say to you, whatever you bind on earth shall be bound in heaven, and whatever you loose on earth shall be loosed in heaven" (Mt 18:18).

In this Sacrament the priest acts *in persona Christi*, that is, "in the person of Christ." While physically we speak to the priest, we are actually speaking directly to Christ. The priest speaks the words, "I absolve you of your sins, in the name of the Father, and of the Son, and of the Holy Spirit." But it is actually God who forgives the penitent at that moment.

Mercy in the Sacrament of Reconciliation flows both from the words we speak and from the words we hear spoken by the priest. In this Sacrament, we are given the opportunity to claim our failures. We speak them out loud and release them from our soul. We ask our Lord for forgiveness. Then we receive our answer from God. We hear the words of absolution. We are assured by God through his minister that we are forgiven. There is no question or lingering doubt. We are forgiven. We have a clean slate. We can begin again.

Anointing of the Sick. Through the Sacrament of the Anointing of the Sick, Christ reaches out in a special way to those in great need of mercy—the sick and elderly, especially those in imminent danger of death. Mindful that these people are prone to self-absorption, despair, or even revolt against God, this Sacrament serves as a reminder of God's great love and his desire to heal, not merely for a moment but for eternity (*CCC*, 1501, 1503).

The actions of this Sacrament are the actions of Christ, the compassionate healer. The minister touches us. He anoints us with oil. He prays for us. He speaks words of comfort and consolation to us.

Through this Sacrament a person's sins are forgiven, "if the sick person was not able to obtain it through the sacrament of Penance" (*CCC*, 1532). This person also receives graces to aid him in the time of trial. These include the spiritual uniting of his sufferings to those of Christ in his Passion; the grace of strength, peace, and courage to endure; and preparation for passing over into eternal life. There is also the grace of restoration to health if such would be conducive to the salvation of one's soul (cf. *CCC*, 1532).

Eucharist. While not always recognized, the Eucharist is a Sacrament from which unfathomable mercy flows. Greater even than the grace imparted by the Eucharist is the mercy that is the reality of the Eucharist itself. The Eucharist is the very Body, Blood, Soul, and Divinity of Jesus Christ. The Eucharist is God. The Eucharist is Mercy Incarnate.

That an infinite God, Creator of the universe, would deign, for our benefit, to be contained in the form of what was once a little white piece of bread is an unfathomable mystery. God gives us his very Body and Blood to eat. He communes with us in the most intimate manner, by entering into us and becoming part of our very being. He does so physically, uniting with our very bodies. And he also does so spiritually, uniting in a supernatural way with our souls.

Through the reception of the Eucharist, our venial sins (those not of a serious nature) are forgiven, we are given special graces that strengthen our resolve to avoid future sin, and we are brought in closer relationship with Christ and the entire Church.

SIX

Showing Mercy

Showing Mercy to Others

When asked to identify the greatest commandment, Jesus replied, "You shall love the Lord, your God, with all your heart, with all your soul, and with all your mind." He then went on to say, "The second is like it: You shall love your neighbor as yourself" (Mt 22:36–49). In directing us to love God and our neighbor, Jesus admonishes us to be merciful.

The second greatest commandment requires us to show mercy to all. We must love our neighbor as ourselves. We must forgive our neighbor's wrongs toward others and toward us. We must overlook our neighbor's shortcomings. We must desire what is best for our neighbor. We must wish our neighbor well. Regardless of how challenging it may be, we must strive to love our neighbor and to show him mercy. And, as we've recognized in the parable of the good samaritan, this includes our enemies and those who persecute us.

To follow the first commandment, we must follow the second. God is love and mercy itself. The very being of God is to show mercy to all, especially to poor sinners. If we are to love God, we must imitate God. As God loves our neighbor and is merciful toward him, we must also love our neighbor and show him mercy.

How could we possibly love God with our whole heart if we hate one of his beloved daughters? How could we love God with our whole mind if we think badly of one of his beloved sons? How could we love God with our whole soul if we failed to show mercy to one of his beloved children? To love God with our whole heart, mind, and soul, we must show mercy to all.

In the Our Father, Jesus taught us to pray the words "forgive us our trespasses as we forgive those who trespass against us." This might also be translated for purposes of our current reflection as "Lord, be merciful to us as we are merciful to others." This phrase of the Our Father contains both an admonition and an assurance. The admonition is that if we wish to receive mercy from God, we must be merciful to others. The assurance is that if we show mercy to others, we can trust that God will be merciful to us.

In the parable of the unmerciful servant, a king wishes to settle accounts with his servants. He learns that a servant owes him a great deal of money, which he cannot repay, and so the king mercifully forgives the servant of his debts. This same servant then goes to a fellow servant who owed him a fraction of the amount that he had owed the king. But despite the fellow servant's pleas, the first servant unmercifully throws him into prison. Upon hearing of the actions of his pardoned servant, the king becomes enraged and hands the first servant over to torturers, exclaiming, "Should you not have had mercy on your fellow servant as I had mercy on you?" (Mt 18:23–33, RSV-2CE).

How can we expect to receive mercy if we ourselves are unmerciful? If we will not show mercy to our neighbors, we should not expect mercy from God. God asks us to show mercy to others because he has first shown us mercy; God asks us to show some small amount of mercy toward our neighbor because he has showered incalculable mercy upon us.

In expecting us to be merciful to others, God places no burden upon us that he has not already undertaken himself a thousand-fold. There is no debt owed to us by a neighbor that compares to the debt God has forgiven man. No neighbor of ours has offended us the way we constantly offend the Almighty. Rather, God has given us everything we are or have. He has suffered and died for us, and he perpetually offers us mercy. In return, God merely asks that we reflect his mercy in our dealings with others.

In the story of the Judgment of the Nations, Jesus explains that each man and woman will have to stand before the throne and be separated "one from another, as a shepherd separates the sheep from the goats." The good "sheep" will be admitted into Heaven for eternal life and the evil "goats" will be banished from God's presence for eternal punishment. To the evil, Jesus will explain that, as they failed to show mercy to his least brother and sister, they failed to show mercy to him (cf. Mt 25:41–46).

In this just judgment, our Lord explains that failing to love our neighbor is failing to love God. Each of us is a beloved child of God. Each of us is equally brother or sister to Jesus; each of us is equally cherished. Both of the great commandments require that we must be merciful to our neighbor. By choosing not to be merciful to our neighbor, we fail to love our neighbor. In choosing not to love our neighbor, we choose not to love our God. The justice of God is that he will allow us to have that which we have chosen freely. If we freely choose to separate ourselves from the love of God here on earth, that separation will be given to us for all eternity.

But let us not dwell too long on the "admonition" contained in the Our Father, for his "assurance" is far greater. If we show mercy to others, God will show mercy to us. And when we do, God will not merely repay us with some equivalent act of mercy but will shower infinite mercy upon us for all eternity! Jesus assures us that even the simplest act of mercy toward "the least" brother or sister of his is an act of love and mercy toward Jesus himself. To us who show mercy to the "least"— anywhere and at any time—Jesus will joyfully proclaim at the end of our lives, "Come, you who are blessed by my Father. Inherit the kingdom prepared for you from the foundation of the world" (Mt 25:34).

In the corporal and spiritual works of mercy, the Church provides us a blueprint for showing mercy to others. These acts of mercy are taken from Scripture, especially from Jesus's account of separating the sheep from the goats. The corporal works of mercy (*corporal* comes from the Latin word for body) address the physical and temporal wellbeing of others. The spiritual works of mercy address the needs of another's soul.

The corporal works of mercy are to

1. feed the hungry,
2. give drink to the thirsty,
3. clothe the naked,
4. visit the imprisoned,
5. shelter the homeless,
6. visit the sick, and
7. bury the dead.

These works are all rather intuitive and most of us have many opportunities to perform them. We can give money to a beggar, donate used clothes, donate to a charity, or volunteer at a soup kitchen or homeless shelter. We can visit someone in the hospital or in prison or volunteer for a jail ministry. We can also make a donation to offset funeral costs incurred by a family of limited means.

Sometimes the corporal works of mercy can be performed in very ordinary, yet no less important ways. We can work in order to earn money to feed our family, make dinner for our children, or bring a drink of water to a spouse who is cutting the grass. We can put up a friend or relative who is in town for a couple of days. We can write to, email, or call someone who is elderly or homebound due to illness. We can drive someone who doesn't have a car to the store. We can attend a wake or funeral, even if we don't know the person well.

However, we are sometimes called to be more heroic in our corporal acts of mercy. We might literally give the coat off our back to a homeless person shivering on a cold day. We might volunteer for a mission trip or start up a ministry that reaches out to a group not actively ministered to in our area. We might become a foster family or welcome into our house, for a period of time, a family that is on the verge of living on the streets. We might take up the care of an ill neighbor who has no family.

The spiritual works of mercy are to

1. admonish the sinner,
2. instruct the ignorant,
3. counsel the doubtful,
4. comfort the sorrowful,
5. bear wrongs patiently,
6. forgive injuries willingly, and
7. pray for the living and the dead.

These are less concrete and perhaps less obvious than the corporal works of mercy in that the effects of our spiritual works of mercy are not readily apparent. Regardless, they are every bit as important as the corporal works.

To admonish sinners and *to instruct the ignorant* are closely related. To admonish sinners is to point out sin in another; to instruct the ignorant is to help another develop the intellect necessary to grow in a healthy manner, especially in the understanding of truth. As this person comes to the truth, he or she will grow in holiness and in the knowledge of good and evil. Parents, teachers, and those in authority over others have the greatest opportunity and responsibility to practice these two spiritual works of mercy.

In an increasingly relativistic world that preaches political correctness and a warped sense of tolerance, these two works of mercy, especially the first, are unpopular. When we tolerate sin, we perform an act that further promotes sin. It is not wrong for us to "judge," if we judge rightly, and if we do so out of love for another person, and so long as our relationship with that person is such that judgment is appropriate. Regardless of the situation, we must be prudent, and we must always speak the truth in love. In fact, we cannot speak the truth without love, and we cannot love without speaking the truth. To admonish sinners is not an act of malicious judgment but of loving mercy.

All of us who are parents must practice these two works of mercy toward our children. Spouses will, if they truly love each other, also practice them, regardless of the temporary pain that may result. Any good friend should also practice these. If such a work of mercy is reasonably calculated to lead to the spiritual growth of another, we should heroically undertake it, despite the temporal cost to ourselves (e.g., the loss of a friendship or job).

To counsel the doubtful does not necessarily mean to give another advice. Often our advice to another stems more from our pride than from selfless love. If we are to counsel the doubtful with advice, we must ensure that our advice is steeped in the truth and given out of pure motive. We counsel the doubtful when we bring another closer to the truth, especially the truth of our Faith. We also counsel the doubtful when we speak words of encouragement or give a warm embrace to another person.

To comfort the afflicted is closely aligned with several of the corporal works of mercy. This spiritual work helps to supercharge the others. It is merciful to drop some money into a beggar's cup, but far more merciful to bend down and chat with the person for a while. It is merciful to give someone money for lunch, but more merciful to sit down and listen to them while they eat. We comfort the afflicted when we not only provide for some physical need, but also connect with them—listen to them, empathize with them, affirm them, and encourage them. There is perhaps no greater comfort we can give to one afflicted than to look them in the eyes and say from our heart, "I love you." This truly reflects the mercy of our Lord.

To bear wrongs patiently and *to forgive offenses willingly* are herculean tasks for all but the most humble saints. "I was wronged" is the automatic cry of our heart when our daughters ignore us, our bosses demean us, our friends gossip about us, or our contractors cheat us. Our pride and our self-centered sense of justice stand in stark contradiction to our desire to bear wrongs patiently and forgive willingly. Yet these are the spiritual works of mercy that Christ personified throughout his ministry, especially in his Passion and Death. To bear wrongs and forgive offenses in love epitomizes the mercy of God; it is to be Christ toward a neighbor.

To pray for the living and the dead is a spiritual work of mercy that is often relegated to a platitude. We often consider prayer for others to be a nice gesture, but one without much worth (unless it is a prayer that somehow benefits us, and then we really put our hearts into it). What a sad, distorted image! Jesus is the model of prayer, and he told us to pray nonstop for everyone—our family and friends, strangers and enemies, and the living and the dead. Even when there seem to be no visible effects, we can be assured that all prayer is heard by God and answered; all prayer is efficacious.

To pray for the living and the dead is our most abundant act of mercy. All of us can show mercy in prayer at any time, under any circumstance. When nothing else can be done for others, especially for the dead, we can always be merciful by praying for them.

Showing Mercy to God

No, the title of this section is not a misprint. We are called to be merciful to God. To most, that will sound rather strange, perhaps impossible. Yet we are, in fact, called to show mercy to God.

Before we address how we can show mercy to God, we must first come to an understanding of an important difference between the mercy we show to another person and the mercy we show to God. As human beings, each one of us needs mercy: We need to be forgiven by others. We need the compassion of others. We need love and support. God, however, does not need anything; he is entirely complete and perfect. But because God loves us, he gives us a beautiful gift—the ability to love him in return and to act lovingly toward him. Therefore, our ability to show God mercy is actually a merciful gift to us from God.

We show mercy to God both indirectly and directly. Indirectly, we show mercy to God by being merciful to others and to ourselves. Jesus assures us that whatever we do for our brothers and sisters, even the least of them, we do for him: "For

I was hungry and you gave *me* food, I was thirsty and you gave *me* drink, a stranger and you welcomed *me*" (Mt 25:35–36, emphasis added). Therefore any mercy shown to another is mercy shown to God.

Directly, we show God mercy when we praise him, thank him, and meditate upon Christ's sufferings, and when we unite our own sufferings to his. St. Paul tells us in his Letter to the Colossians, "Now I rejoice in my sufferings for your sake, and in my flesh I am filling up what is lacking in the afflictions of Christ on behalf of his body, which is the church" (Col 1:24). At first, this might seem like a contradiction. Christ is the perfect, unblemished sacrifice and God almighty. There is nothing that Jesus failed to do in order to accomplish his gift of salvation. There is no amount of suffering that he could not bear or refused to bear on our behalf. There is no further activity he failed to perform or needs us to undertake in order for him to complete his work here on earth. Yet he chose to leave work to be done by us, for our own good.

The only thing that is "lacking" in the sufferings of Christ is our cooperation in his suffering. In love, God gave us the choice to accept or reject the saving power of Christ's Passion, Death, and Resurrection. In love, God gave us the opportunity to share in Christ's Passion. In love, God gave us the ability to take up Christ's suffering for our own good and the good of the entire body of Christ, that is, the Church.

Christ admonishes us to take up our crosses—our own version of Christ's Cross—and follow him. Just as God allowed Simon of Cyrene to help Christ carry his Cross literally, so too does he allow us to assist him. Could not Christ have cast off his mortal constraints and carried it himself? Certainly! Or, could not the Father have sent a host of angels to bear it for him? Undoubtedly! But God loves us so much that he humbled himself and accepted the assistance of man.

Christ completed, once and for all, the perfect sacrifice on Calvary. But, every day, every one of us is faced with the decision to accept or reject the salvation offered. Every day there is something lacking that needs to be filled. Every day we have the opportunity to join Christ in his work for the salvation of souls—our souls and the souls of all of our brothers and sisters.

Just before Jesus died on the Cross, he said, "I thirst." Someone took a sponge soaked in wine and, on a stick, placed it to Jesus's lips. After taking the wine, Jesus expired (cf. Jn 19:28–30). The very last act of Christ before dying was an invitation for a small act of mercy to be rendered to him. In saying, "I thirst," Jesus was not merely referring to the very real dehydration caused by his suffering and loss of blood, but also his thirst for souls. Jesus thirsts for every soul and invites each and every one to come and receive the saving waters of his mercy.

Jesus thirsts for us. He thirsts that we might be saved. He thirsts that we might be compassionately drawn into his suffering. He thirsts that we might desire in love to reach out and satiate his thirst. And Jesus thirsts that we might continue to make up what is lacking in his sufferings—to reach out daily and satiate the thirst of all the members of his Body.

Suffering comes to each of us in many different forms at many different times throughout our lives. We suffer in small and big ways, emotionally, physically, and spiritually. It is unavoidable and distasteful, but it is also very useful because suffering is a means to grow closer to God.

It is hard to suffer. We feel not only the normal physical or emotional pain that results from the cause of our suffering, but also isolation, depression, anxiety, and despair. It is hard to pray while we suffer. Perhaps we feel abandoned by God or our pain is just so great that we can't focus on anything. This is exactly why prayer in suffering is such a gift by us to God.

"Offer it up" has been a common statement of pastors to their flocks and parents to their children for the last several generations. It admonishes us to offer up our sufferings to God intentionally, as prayer for others, especially for the poor souls in Purgatory. This practice is a beautiful and effective means of advancing the Kingdom of God here on earth.

To offer up one's suffering is particularly merciful because we look outward toward the good of another at a time when it would be natural to look inward and become self-absorbed. The natural tendency is to try to run from suffering, which is generally impossible, or to "gut through it." While we need not desire that the suffering continue, it is by accepting our suffering and offering it up for others that God's mercy is extended.

Let us imagine the following words of Isaiah coming from Christ on the Cross: "Insult has broken my heart, and I despair; I looked for compassion, but there was none, for comforters, but found none" (Is 69:21). Every day, we have the opportunity to show Christ compassion and to comfort him by lovingly accepting the sufferings that come our way and by uniting them to his Passion. Every day we can make up what is lacking in his sufferings by offering up our sufferings for the good of our neighbor and the salvation of souls. As we receive mercy from God, we too can show him mercy in return.

Showing Mercy to Ourselves

The two great commandments—(1) to love God with our whole heart, mind, and strength, and (2) to love our neighbor as ourselves—are often not fully appreciated. Unfortunately these commandments are often understood to mean only that we are to love God and our neighbor. But such an interpretation leaves out a person who very much needs our love—our self.

God calls us to love our neighbor *as ourselves*. If we seek to love our neighbor while not loving ourselves, we obviously fail to follow this command. Furthermore, if we fail to love ourselves, we're not showing true love of God. He loves each and every one of us. How could we possibly claim to love him with our whole heart, mind, and strength if we fail to love one of his cherished sons and daughters (ourselves)?

Our deepest identity is that we are beautiful, beloved sons and daughters of our Almighty Father. He created us and loves us exactly as we are. He loves our hair color, eyes, wrinkles, and moles. He loves us despite all of our faults and imperfections. He loves us even when we fail to love him in return. Despite *any* sin we have *ever* committed, God continues to love us and offer us his mercy. And just as he is merciful toward us, so too must we be merciful to ourselves!

We must look at ourselves through the merciful eyes of our Lord. We must recognize that all of the sins we have confessed are completely forgiven. We must recognize that all of our self-perceived character flaws and failings are redeemed through the mercy of God. We must also recognize that, just as God has mercy on us, we must have mercy on ourselves. We must claim for ourselves the mercy of God; we must cry out from our inmost being, "Through God's mercy I have been saved, through God's mercy I am being saved, and through God's mercy I will be saved!"

SEVEN

Mary, Mother of Mercy

Literally

Throughout the history of the Church, Mary has been revered for her special association with God's mercy. And many of her titles are associated with mercy: Mother of Mercy, Our Lady of Mercy, Queen of Mercy, and Virgin Most Merciful. Additionally, Mary is invoked as "Refuge of Sinners," "Comforter of the Afflicted," and "Help of Christians." It is important to understand that these titles are not merely honorific; they are accurate descriptions of Mary's role in God's plan of salvation.

Mary is *literally* the mother of Mercy. She is the human mother of our Lord Jesus Christ who is Mercy Incarnate. Sin entered into the world through Adam and Eve. The mercy of salvation entered into the world though the new Adam, Christ, and the new Eve, Mary.

God showed a special mercy to Mary in her Immaculate Conception: from the moment of her conception, Mary was preserved from the stain of Original Sin. Mary was also preserved from concupiscence—the tendency to sin—that each of us inherits from the Fall of Adam and Eve.

Like the original Eve, Mary, the new Eve, was conceived without sin. And like the original Eve, Mary was endowed with free will and the ability to sin. Unlike Eve, however, Mary remained inviolate, ceaselessly conforming her will to God's.

Because of her sin, Eve gave birth to mankind bound by sin. Because of her fidelity, Mary gave birth to the Mercy of God, the remedy for sin, Jesus Christ; and through Mary all of mankind has been spiritually reborn through the salvation won by her Son. Hence, the new Eve has given birth to mankind not bound by sin, but free through the mercy of God.

Even though few facts are recorded about Mary's life in the Bible, the few that exist exhibit Mary's heroic mercy. She consented to conceive a child, though not through union with Joseph, her betrothed. By trusting in God, she subjected herself to the possibility of being put to death for perceived adultery. Immediately upon conceiving, she looked not to her own needs, but to the needs of her kinswoman, Elizabeth, who was pregnant with St. John the Baptist.

Mary never faltered in her complete submission to God's will, despite Simeon's dire prediction of the suffering she would endure and the piercing of her heart. At the Wedding Feast at Cana, Mary encouraged Jesus to perform his first public miracle, even though it meant the beginning of his public ministry and his journey toward inevitable death.

When almost all had abandoned Jesus, Mary stayed by his side and shared in his Passion. Spiritually, Mary felt the blows of his scourging, helped bear his Cross along the path to Golgotha, and suffered with him as he lay stretched out dying on the Cross. Mary's Immaculate Heart was pierced just as

Jesus's Most Sacred Heart was pierced with a lance. Mary, the Mother of Mercy, perfectly united her sufferings to those of her Son for the sake of our souls.

To better understand the depths of the mercy of Mary, we might meditate upon the following words by Fr. Eddie Doherty.

> Was ever a woman placed in such a situation, that she must pray, that she must hope to see the death of Him she loves with all her heart—and must rejoice when He is dead—because of her love for those who slay him?[1]

Our Merciful Mother

In his words from the Cross, which he spoke to St. John, "Behold your Mother," our Lord gave his mother to us all. From both the unbroken tradition of the Church and from the inspiration of saints and mystics, we know that from the very beginning of the Church, Mary was her merciful mother. She cared for the Apostles, strengthened them, and guided them.

Mary was the quiet, constant source of strength throughout Christ's Passion, Death, Resurrection, and Ascension. When the faith of the Apostles was tested, Mary's never wavered. Mary was a source of strength that kept the Apostles together until, empowered by the Holy Spirit, they were ready to take on their roles of leadership and evangelize the world.

Following Our Lady's Assumption into Heaven, her role as our mother did not end, but was perfected; she took her

---

[1] Eddie Doherty, *Splendor of Sorrow* (Manchester, New Hampshire: Sophia Institute Press, 2002), p. 71.

place as "Queen of Heaven and Earth." The earliest Church Fathers (e.g., Sts. Irenaeus, Ephrem, Cyril of Alexandria, etc.), the founders of the great religious orders (e.g., Sts. Benedict, Ignatius, Francis, Dominic, etc.), and modern day saints (e.g., Sts. Maximilian Kolbe, John Paul II, Teresa of Calcutta, etc.) have all recognized the singular role of Mary as our maternal mediator before the throne of God.

The Second Vatican Council recognized Mary's maternal role in the order of grace through her titles "Advocate, Auxiliatrix, Adjutrix, and Mediatrix."[2] While neither taking away nor adding to the efficaciousness of Christ the one Mediator, Mary cooperated fully with God through her constant obedience to God's will and through her faith, hope, and burning charity. She graciously accepted all that came her way, including every suffering, and she united herself, with perfect compassion, to her Son as he died on the Cross. Accordingly, not out of necessity but out of his love for us, our Lord gave his mother to be our constant intercessor.[3]

There is an old Latin adage *lex orandi, lex credendi*, which is translated, "as we pray, so we believe." This adage captures the fact that the way we pray forms what we believe. This saying is particularly true in reference to the unwavering understanding of Mary's role as our merciful Mother. So many of the prayers of the Church, including the most ancient and those most frequently prayed, call upon Mary's intercession. They especially request her intercession in obtaining the ultimate

---

[2] *Lumen Gentium*, (November 21, 1965), no. 62.
[3] Ibid, 60–62.

mercy—forgiveness of sins and everlasting life in Heaven. While there are countless prayers calling upon the merciful intercession of Mary, a few deserve special mention.

The *Hail Mary* invokes Mary with the words "pray for us sinners, now and at the hour of our death." We pray for Mary's special intercession, not only for our daily needs, but also for the final grace of Heaven. We ask Mary to petition on our behalf that our Lord will be merciful to us upon our death and welcome us into the eternal reward of Heaven.

The *Hail Holy Queen*, which is sung in the Night Prayer of the Liturgy of the Hours, and typically prayed at the end of the Rosary, beseeches the mercy of Mary as follows:

> Hail, Holy Queen, Mother of Mercy, our life, our sweetness and our hope. To you do we cry, poor banished children of Eve. To you do we send up our sighs, mourning and weeping in this valley of tears. Turn then, most gracious Advocate, your eyes of mercy towards us, and after this exile show unto us the blessed fruit of your womb, Jesus. O clement, O loving, O sweet Virgin Mary. Pray for us, O holy Mother of God. That we may be made worthy of the promises of Christ.

In this prayer, we invoke Mary specifically as "Mother of Mercy." We recognize that we are sinners, justly banished from the Garden of Eden. We admit that by our nature, we are the children of the first Eve, inclined to sin, subject to pain and sadness, and destined for the grave. But, we now turn to Mary as the new Eve, our spiritual mother. We ask her intercession that we might, through grace, obtain the glorious reward promised by Jesus to those who love him. We sing out with joy in the fact that Mary is sweet, loving, clement, and merciful. We sing out these praises knowing that she will do all in her power to obtain that which we ask.

Another ancient prayer that acknowledges the great efficacy of Mary's intercessory power is the *Memorare*:

> Remember, O most gracious Virgin Mary, that never was it known that anyone who fled to your protection, implored your help, or sought your intercession was left unaided. Inspired with this confidence, I fly unto you, O Virgin of virgins, my Mother. To you do I come, before you I stand, sinful and sorrowful. O Mother of the Word Incarnate, despise not my petitions, but in your mercy hear and answer me.

Once again, we have a prayer that acknowledges our sinfulness and the sorrow that results from it. Despite our unworthiness, we pray in confidence that God will forgive our sins, that we will be protected, and that our needs will be met. *Never was it known* that our Mother of Mercy failed to grant any request made for our true good.

There is a beautiful prayer called the *Litany of the Blessed Virgin Mary* or the "Litany of Loreto," approved for public use by Pope Sixtus V in 1587. In this prayer, Mary is invoked by many titles and, under each individual title, is asked to pray for us. Several of these titles particularly highlight Mary's role in obtaining mercy for us. She is invoked as Virgin Most Merciful, Health of the Sick, Refuge of Sinners, Comforter of the Afflicted, Help of Christians, and Gate of Heaven.

Mary's ongoing role as our Mother of Mercy is further highlighted by her many apparitions over the centuries and those occurring today. In times of great tribulation and need, our Mother assures us of the mercy of God and promises to intercede for us.

In 1531, Mary revealed herself as "merciful mother" to St. Juan Diego and to all people who love her and cry out to her for help. Mary assured Juan Diego that she always hears our weeping and sorrows and will remedy all of our sufferings and needs.[4]

In 1917, Mary appeared to three young shepherds in Fatima, Portugal. Mary showed them a terrible vision of Hell, but promised to intercede for everyone's salvation: "If people do what I tell you, many will be saved, and peace will come. I promise to help at the hour of death with the graces for their salvation."[5]

In the 1980s, Mary appeared to three children in the small town of Kibeho. During this time leading up to the Rwanda genocide, a culture of evil and hostility toward God and religion was festering. Mary appeared and revealed her concern for the people, saying, "What I ask of you is repentance. ...Today, many people do not know any more how to ask forgiveness. They nail again the Son of God on the Cross."[6] But Mary promised that the strength to repent would be given to those who would meditate on Mary's own sorrows, united to those of Christ.

There have been many more apparitions—both those officially recognized by the Church and those still under

---

[4] Francis Johnson, *The Wonder of Guadalupe* (Charlotte, North Carolina: Tan Books, 1981), pp. 26–27.

[5] http://fatima.ageofmary.com/overview/.

[6] http://www.michaeljournal.org/kibeho.htm.

investigation. In all of these apparitions, Mary constantly reveals her tender, maternal concern for all our temporal and eternal needs. These apparitions further reveal her role as merciful mediator. Mary's words to St. Brigid of Sweden are particularly poignant: "I am the Queen of Heaven and the Mother of Mercy; I am the joy of the just, and the door through which sinners are brought to God."[7]

Our Lady, Mother of Mercy,

Pray for us!

---

[7] Rev. 1.6, c.10.

PART II

HOPE

Hope, O my soul, hope. You know neither the day nor the hour. Watch carefully, for everything passes quickly, even though your impatience makes doubtful what is certain, and turns a very short time into a long one. Dream that the more you struggle, the more you prove the love that you bear your God, and the more you will rejoice one day with your Beloved, in a happiness and rapture that can never end. (St. Teresa of Ávila, Excl. 15:3.)

ONE

Understanding Hope

A Realistic Expectation

What is hope? And how do we attain hope, which we so greatly desire, yet find so elusive? Is hope a feeling? Is it a state of being? Yes, it is both of these things and so much more. Can we find hope if we desire it? Can hope find us even if we aren't actively seeking it? Yes, hope is both a freely given gift and also something that results from our own actions. Hope is a desire of our heart that is assured of its fulfillment. It is a realistic expectation—an expectation accompanied by the knowledge that the expectation will be met.

Hope is a challenging concept because it is multifaceted. Hope is a virtue, a feeling, and an action. Ideally, all three of these facets would work in concert at all times within us to bring about true and perfect hope. Realistically, we often ignore the virtue, obsess over the feeling, and fail to take any action toward living in hope.

The virtue of hope. Hope is first and foremost a virtue, more specifically, a theological virtue. Though related, there is a great distinction between what we generally refer to as a *virtue* and what the Church defines as a *theological virtue.*

A virtue is commonly understood as a behavior exhibiting moral quality. *The Catechism of the Catholic Church* defines a virtue, similarly, as "a habitual and firm disposition to do the good."[1] There are numerous virtues. Some are considered so important for the moral life that they are referred to as *cardinal virtues*. The Latin root of the word *cardinal* means hinge or pivot, which helps describe these virtues as being pivotal for developing the other virtues. The cardinal virtues are prudence, justice, fortitude, and temperance. Other virtues include humility, kindness, honesty, courage, generosity, patience, respectfulness, and gratitude, just to name a few.

Theological virtues are defined as "gifts infused by God into the souls of the faithful to make them capable of acting as his children and of meriting eternal life."[2] There are only three theological virtues: faith, hope, and charity (alternately referred to as "love").

The greatest distinction between a moral virtue and a theological virtue is how it arises in a soul. Moral virtues are usually acquired through at least some human activity, though God might give us a disposition prone to a certain virtue. He also constantly gives us grace that bolsters a virtue. However, regardless of how much assistance God gives us, to a great extent, we grow in specific virtues through our daily effort. We practice patience, we endeavor to be courageous, and we work at humility.

---

[1] *CCC* Glossary, p. 903.
[2] Ibid.

While moral virtues are acquired greatly through our effort, theological virtues are pure gifts from God. They are not earned or obtained, rather they are infused into our souls at Baptism. But we must still respond to them. We must desire them and cooperate with their action in our lives in order for us to experience them fully.

Hope is the theological virtue by which we desire Heaven and trust that we will obtain Heaven. Infusing hope into our souls, God has gifted us with the knowledge that Heaven will be the fulfillment of all of our desires: It will be eternal joy and peace. It will be perfect eternal communion with the Blessed Trinity and all our brothers and sisters. It will also be the perfection of all of our imperfections—a wholeness of mind, body, and soul. But hope is not the desire for an unobtainable end. Rather, it is the virtue by which God assures us that he will give us every grace needed to obtain our perfect end.

Hope guides us through the darkness. It assures us of the light that is just beyond our sight. Hope assures us that God loves us, that we are his children, and that his gaze is ever fixed on us, even if we cannot perceive it. Hope sustains us through trials and strengthens us in our weakness. Hope assures us of our end.

We do not deserve the theological virtue of hope. It is pure gift from God. Nor can we earn more of this virtue. Rather, as baptized Christians, we have all the hope we need. But, as we will discuss shortly, we are called to embrace hope and act in conformity with it. The effect of this cooperation with grace will lead to constant growth in our relationship with God.

The virtue of hope, although given to us by God, does not negate our free will because we can freely reject this virtue. Hope is, in effect, an assurance by God that he will be our guide throughout our journey here on earth. He will never leave our side. He will lead us to the gate of Heaven and hold it open for us. But, we must choose to follow him, and choose to enter through the opened gate: "So far as God's part is concerned, our Salvation is certain. It is only our part—our cooperation or non-cooperation with God's grace—that is uncertain."[3]

A feeling of hope. Despite the ever-present virtue of hope, it is appropriate to recognize that hope is also a feeling. In fact, taken out of context of its spiritual reality, hope is generally defined solely as a feeling. As a feeling, hope is commonly understood as an expectation and desire for a certain thing to happen: We hope that the sun will rise tomorrow. We hope that we will pass the final exam. We hope that the biopsy results will be negative. All of these examples of hope are similar in that they all express a desire for something. They do not, however, all produce the same feeling of expectation.

As we go to sleep, we fully expect that the world will not come to an end, but that the sun will rise the following morning; so we drift off in peace and surety. If we have failed every test and quiz during the semester, our hope for success on the final is thin and uncomforting. We desire success, but do not expect it. Our hope does not calm our anxiety. As we await the results of our skin biopsy, our hope might vary from

---

[3] Leo J. Trese, *The Faith Explained* (Philippines: Sinag-Tala, 1983), p. 106.

day to day or even moment to moment, and it is influenced by so many other factors, both under our control and out of our control: our family history, the amount of time we have spent in the sun, the appearance of the spot, and the reaction of our physician.

The virtue of hope, however, is not a feeling; it is an assurance. But it is met with feelings on our part. God has given us a desire for Heaven, and he has assured us that we can obtain Heaven. And yet, it is understandable and very human to feel, at least at times, less than assured and, sometimes, down-right hopeless.

Because of sin, our intellect is clouded and our emotions are distorted. In our inmost being, we know that God loves us and created us for eternal communion with him. No other possibility makes sense. Yet, we don't always feel God's presence; we don't always feel his love; and we don't always feel that we will obtain the goal for which we are destined. But our feelings don't change reality.

The key to hope is to acknowledge our feelings and separate them from reality. If we do not feel the hope of Heaven, we must recognize that these feelings are natural but false. God does love us! We are beautifully created! We are destined for eternal joy! Conversely, even when we feel God's pleasure, we must recognize that these feelings are a gift from God and not a condition for obtaining the glory that awaits us.

The act of hope. Hope is not only a virtue and a feeling, but also an action. The infusion of the virtue of hope within us is not enough; we must act in hope. Whether or not we feel hopeful, we must act in hope.

Hope is a response. God infuses us with the sure knowledge that we are destined for glory. God fills us with every grace necessary to obtain the joy of Heaven. And God gives us free will. We are free to accept or reject our birthright. We are free to use the tools he gives us or to cast them aside and wander aimlessly toward oblivion.

God acts, and then we respond. God leads the way, and then we decide whether to follow. God has already completed the work of salvation through his Incarnation, Passion, Death, and Resurrection. All graces necessary for our personal salvation flow from this act of God. Yet we must respond to God's salvific action. We must cooperate with his plan.

Let's imagine we are hiking up a mountain toward Heaven. God is our outfitter and guide. He gives us boots and a map. He cuts the trail ahead of us and walks besides us. When we slip, he throws us a rope. The virtue of hope assures us the boots will provide the traction we need, the map will point us in the right direction, and the rope will not break. But we must act. We must put on the boots. We must look at the map. We must grasp the rope. Our feelings of hope along the journey may come and go. Sometimes we will feel we are on the right path and other times, quite lost. Sometimes we will see God leading the way and other times feel abandoned. But regardless of how we feel, we must act. We must keep climbing.

Hope is a decision. In fact, the most important "act" of hope involves no external activity whatsoever. Rather, the first and foremost act of hope is to accept hope. It is the decision to say "Yes" to God; it is the decision to trust God.

In hope, we decide to accept God's love, despite any feelings of love that we have or lack thereof. We decide to trust in his plan for us, even when we feel lost. In hope, we trust that all of the pain and heartaches that we experience throughout life are not without merit or reason and we will be infinitely compensated for them by the joys of Heaven. In hope, we decide on a destiny and trust that we will arrive.

A realistic expectation. Hope is not mere wishful thinking or a false assurance of a pleasant future; it is not a dream or a comforting distraction. Hope neither depends on our inconstant emotions, nor our ability to obtain anything for ourselves. Rather, hope is the realistic expectation of an end more glorious than we can imagine.

Faith and Hope

In our efforts to better understand and embrace hope, it will be helpful for us to recognize the relationship between hope and faith. In common parlance, hope and faith are sometimes used almost interchangeably. But, while they are closely related and complementary, these two virtues are also separate and distinct. And, as we tend to focus more frequently on faith, we can often lose sight of the importance of embracing hope.

Faith and hope are both theological virtues. They are both gifts infused into the soul by God. They are unearned, they remain in the soul eternally, and they both require a response from us. Both of these virtues have the same goal—that we obtain eternal joy in communion with God in Heaven. But, both work differently within the soul to bring about this end.

Faith is commonly defined as confidence or trust in a belief that is not based on proof. While not completely inapposite to how we must understand faith, this definition is misleading to the extent that it suggests that there is no proof whatsoever or reasonable basis for faith. In fact, everything we accept in faith is reasonable and is based in truth. But, in faith we accept the truth of things we have not personally witnessed and things we cannot fully understand.

Through the supernatural gift of faith, God infuses into our souls the ability to believe what he reveals. In the course of history, God has revealed things to us that we could not come to know by our intellect alone (e.g., that God is a Trinity of three Persons) and things that would be very difficult to come to know (e.g., God loves us and desires to be in personal relationship with us). In faith, we are then invited to embrace these truths revealed by God.

Faith is the free assent to the truth of something despite our inability to understand it fully and despite whether it is within the ability of anyone to fully understand it. Faith is not, however, a belief in something false. Rather, faith complements reason, and, at the same time, exceeds intellectual capacity. We as the Church come to know certain truths not because we have figured them out, but because God has revealed these truths and guides the Church in recognizing them through the gift of faith.

In faith, we believe that Jesus rose from the dead. We did not witness his Resurrection. Nor have we experienced any human condition that did not end in death. Regardless, we believe. And our faith in the Resurrection is reasonable given the Gospel accounts, the witness of the lives of the Apostles, the transformation of the world brought about by Christianity, etc.

The term "blind faith" has no place in our understanding of faith. It would suggest that, in faith, we wander around aimlessly. St. Paul remarks, "We walk by faith, not by sight" (2 Cor 5:7). But he does not mean our faith is *blind*. Our faith is illuminated by absolute truth. Faith is a surer guide than sight. Navigating by sight relies on our own abilities, while navigating by faith relies on God.

We must come, therefore, to the understanding that faith is not so much *belief* as it is *trust*. We don't *believe* that God loves us as if the opposite were possible. Rather, we trust that God loves us. Here is where faith and hope meet.

In faith, we assent to all the truths God has revealed to us. In hope, we trust that these truths are good, for our good, and for the good of all creation. In faith, we trust that God created us out of love and for relationship with him. In hope, we trust that we have already begun an eternal loving relationship with God. In faith, we trust that God created us to be happy. In hope, we trust that we will be eternally happy with God. In faith, we trust that we are designed to attain Heaven. In hope, we trust that we will attain Heaven.

Imagine our time on earth as a car ride toward Heaven. In faith, we trust that God made us, that God made the car, and that God is driving the car. In hope, we trust that if we remain in that car, we will get to Heaven. From God's perspective, our arrival in Heaven is certain. From our perspective, we must trust in God's guidance and not jump out.

In both faith and hope, man encounters God. God reaches out to us personally and gives us the ability to reach back. God reveals himself to us, and he reveals us to ourselves. God gives us the ability to trust in that which we could not trust through our own natural strength. God implants a natural desire to receive his enlightenment and accept his offer of friendship. He offers eternal joy, and then lovingly and patiently waits for our response.

Hope Brings Happiness

Deep within our hearts is the desire for happiness. Perhaps we take this fact for granted. Or, perhaps we fight this natural desire because we incorrectly believe that we are not meant to be happy here on earth. But the fact is, we are supposed to be happy. God wants us to be happy. He created us for happiness. However, we can't take happiness for granted but must work for it. And to be happy, we must embrace hope.

We must dispel the myth that we can't or shouldn't be happy here on earth. To do so, we must recognize that the word happiness often has connotations (and denotations) other than true happiness. We describe ourselves as *happy* when someone gives us a chocolate bar or when our team wins a game. This type of happiness is superficial, fleeting, and a mere shadow of the happiness God desires for us. The happiness that we feel on our wedding day or at the birth of our child is happiness much closer to the mark, yet even these forms of happiness fall short of what God has in store for us.

The happiness God desires for us is the complete, pure, selfless, fulfilling, unbroken, eternal joy that we will experience in Heaven. While not completely obtainable here on earth, this happiness is reflected in the love we feel for a spouse, the wonder we feel as we gaze into a starry sky, and the relief we feel when our child is cured. The happiness God desires for us is even reflected in pain. We are happy as our child goes off to college, even though we feel the loss of her presence, and this is because our desire for her good brings us more happiness than our selfish desire for our own comfort.

We must remove from our minds an unrealistic picture of saints as glum, self-flagellating uber-ascetics. Saints are saints because they truly love God. True love brings true joy. St. John Paul II lived through World War II and the Soviet occupation of Poland, yet he was incredibly joyful. The twinkle in his eye and the smile on his face were ever-present. St. Teresa of Calcutta watched people die of disease and malnutrition every day, yet she remained joyful and high-spirited. Do you think that people gave away all they had and followed St. Francis because he gloomily begged for food and slept on rocks? How absurd! People followed St. Francis because he found joy in everything, even begging for food and sleeping on rocks. What is it in these saints that transformed typically perceived depressing circumstances into happy ones? Hope.

Hope assures us of the perfect storybook ending to our lives, "And we lived happily ever after." In hope we know that our *happily ever after* will come in Heaven, where we will be perfectly and eternally happy. But this assurance of our future joy is only the beginning of the happiness that is imparted by hope. Through hope, we find happiness here on earth as well.

Hope brings happiness by giving us purpose. Hope assures us that there is meaning to our lives and that we are on a path that leads us to God. Hope inspires our daily activities. It reminds us that even the most menial task performed in love can be a prayer that brings us closer to God and Heaven. It keeps us from discouragement by assuring us that our pure intention is greater than the result. Hope focuses our attention on God throughout the day, reminding us of what is important and identifying what is truly eternal in our lives.

Hope brings happiness by opening us to receive love. It assures us that the perfect love of God is the only thing that can bring true eternal happiness. And hope assures us that we are made in love and for love, by God. Hope dispels the doubts of being unworthy of God's love. It assures us that God is madly and passionately in love with us and that he wants to wrap us in his love for all eternity.

Hope brings happiness by helping us to see things in their right order. Hope identifies Heaven as our perfect and obtainable goal. Focusing us on the eternal, hope helps us to discern that which brings true happiness from those things that will bring only fleeting pleasure.

Hope brings happiness by consoling us in times of sadness. Pain, suffering, and death are a part of our lives, and we will feel loss and abandonment. But hope assures us that not only will these things pass, but also that good can come from them. Hope inspires us to offer up the pain of an illness in order to grow closer to God. Hope enables us to forgive an abusive spouse and desire God's forgiveness for him or her as well. Hope enables us to cry tears of joy at the funeral of our father as we envision him at home with our Lord. And hope assures us that no matter how empty and alone we feel, God is still present; he still loves us and is concerned for us, and he is still leading us to eternal joy with him in Heaven.

More so than faith, and even love, hope is the virtue that imparts the greatest happiness here on earth. Faith reveals the reason for happiness, but does not itself impart that happiness. In love we experience happiness, but only to the extent our current broken human nature allows. Hope, however, magnifies the happiness imparted through love by the knowledge that this happiness will not fail but increase infinitely. Further, hope provides happiness in the absence of the experience of love through the sure knowledge of the perfect, eternal love that we will experience in Heaven.

TWO

The Need for Hope

Our Joy Is Not Found Here

It's a good thing that hope brings happiness, because we're not going to find true happiness without it. That is because our true joy can't be found in anything here on earth. Early in our discussion of mercy, we recognized the serious results of Original Sin. We are broken creatures born into a broken world. Because the world is broken, nothing in the world is perfect, and therefore nothing is capable of fully satisfying us. Additionally, because we are broken, we are incapable of being fully satisfied. But even worse, because of our brokenness, we even desire things that make us *un*happy! To paraphrase St. Paul, because of sin I do what I don't want to do, and I don't do what I want to do (cf. Rom 7:18–20).

Because of sin, we sometimes seek happiness in things that by their very nature can't bring us true happiness and, in fact, will eventually cause us great pain. Heroin and other hard-core drugs may offer a few seemingly blissful moments. Then they kill us. Pornography, adultery, and other aberrant sexual behavior may provide short physical "highs"; meanwhile, they distort our view of sexuality, render a meaningful and satisfying physical relationship difficult or impossible, ruin our marriages, and cause serious damage to our souls as well. And these acts become less pleasurable as their frequency increases.

We are also attracted to more mundane things that cause us unhappiness—bad relationships, unhealthy work environments, smoking, binge eating, etc. Even things that are potentially good provide us with only a limited amount of happiness. And, the more we look to these things for our true and lasting happiness, the less happy we will become. No job can make up for the loss of a family. The pleasure of constant over-indulgence in food gives way quickly to serious health issues. Continually buying a better car, house, or other possessions just leaves us emptier and hungrier for the next purchase.

In truth, even the greatest goods here on earth can't make us completely happy. The loving relationships between a husband and wife, a parent and child, and two friends are beautiful reflections of the very love of the Trinity. But none of these relationships are perfect: In the healthiest of marriages, spouses hurt each other. The most loving parents and children bring each other pain. The best of friends cause each other great sadness.

Even our desire to love God and our efforts to grow closer to him won't make us perfectly happy here on earth. We might get bored during a homily or feel anxious during prayer. We might be ill-treated by a priest or parish leader. We might even experience great spiritual dryness or feel abandoned by God. But this is where hope comes to the rescue. Hope provides a great amount of happiness here on earth and assures us of true, eternal happiness in Heaven.

No amount of food we stuff into our mouth will bring us pleasure beyond the grave. The house, car, and bank account will all get left behind. The flattery of others and the cosmetic surgery might have fooled us for a while, but our naked souls will stand before the throne of judgment. None of these fleeting things will bring us joy past this life. But every prayer, every act of love, every kindness toward another, every desire for Heaven will ultimately result in complete, absolute, eternal happiness.

No God, No Hope

Without God, there is no true hope. For the atheist, this world is all there is. Sorrow and pain are valueless nuisances. Moments of happiness are fleeting and unfulfilling. Everything in between is a mixture of monotony and tedium. The agnostic doesn't fare much better. She is open to the possibility that there is something more. Therefore she might hope—that is, she might *desire* that life has meaning and that some ultimate happiness awaits her. But this is not really hope, as there is no realistic expectation. For the believer, however, life is full of hope. The pain and tedium are useful tools to grow in holiness. The mundane is a quiet co-existence with his loving God. His joy is a tiny hint of the ecstasy that awaits him.

There can be no hope without God because we are made for God and nothing else can fulfill us. St. Augustine proclaims, "You have made us for yourself, O Lord, and our heart is restless until it rests in you."[1] Or in more colloquial terms,

---

[1] St. Augustine, *Confessions*, Book 1, paragraph 1.

"We have a God-shaped hole in our hearts and nothing but God can fill it."

We claim to be many things that describe only small portions of our identity: I'm a blond. I'm an Italian. I'm a Chicago Bears fan. I'm a pharmacist. I'm a wife. While any of these might be accurate, they don't reveal our true identity. Rather, our deepest identity is that we are each a beloved child of God.

We try to fill that hole in our hearts with all sorts of things. We try food, alcohol, sports, movies, video games, etc. But the hole remains. We continue to be unsatisfied. We fail to experience true happiness. This is because only God can fill that hole. Only God can complete us.

We are defined by our relationship with God: He created us. He sustains us. He desires everything good for us. He offers to be in a perfect eternal loving relationship with us. And yet, God also honors our individuality. He does not negate our individuality but perfects it. We can still love pizza and love God. We can be football fans and beloved children of God. But more important is to understand the right order of our desires, an order in which God comes first.

There are many wonderful things to experience here on earth: a gorgeous sunset, the vastness of the ocean, the smile of a newborn, the grandeur of a symphony, etc. But all of these are fleeting; it is impossible to stop and eternally immerse ourselves in any of these. They are merely hints of God and are not his fullness.

St. Paul states, "For here we have no lasting city, but we seek the one that is to come" (Heb 13:14). We are not living in our permanent home. Rather, we are on a journey. We have a definite destination. The journey is, at times, wonderful; at other times, quite challenging. But regardless of how beautiful any oasis might be along the way, or how treacherous any path we tread might be, we must press on with the sure knowledge that we will arrive in the heavenly city of God.

We Groan…But Not Forever

In describing our current condition, St. Paul observes that "all creation is groaning… [we] groan within ourselves as we wait for adoption, the redemption of our bodies" (Rom 8:22–23). In this, he acknowledges that there is a lot of pain and suffering here on earth. We live in an imperfect world. Our bodies, minds, and emotions are imperfect. Our relationships are imperfect. The entire created world is imperfect. We are a far cry from the perfect joy we anticipate in Heaven.

Although St. Paul acknowledges our sorrow, he recognizes that our hope is greater: "I consider that the sufferings of this present time are as nothing compared with the glory to be revealed for us" (Rom 8:18). In fact, he likens our current groaning to labor pains. Our pain is real. At times it is intense. We fear it will never end. We are scared of the outcome. But St. Paul assures us that our pain will end and that a new and glorious life awaits us. And, like a woman who has given birth, all of our past pain will be completely forgotten in light of the joy we will experience.

This is a time of waiting. It is filled with both sadness and joy. Sometimes we find ourselves groaning, while at other times we find ourselves rejoicing. Regardless, it is a time of waiting for something far better. We must not focus too much on the pain. The pain will pass away, never to return. We must not become satisfied with the fleeting joy. It, too, will pass, but will be replaced with infinitely more joy.

Our waiting and groaning must not, however, amount to lingering and despairing. We are not caught in some endless limbo. Rather, we are called to move forward toward a specific destination. Despite how far our objective might seem, we are assured that we will arrive. Despite the challenges we face along the way, the journey will be well worth it.

St. Paul enjoins us to "rejoice in hope, endure in affliction, [and] persevere in prayer" (Rom 12:12). While all three of these are challenging, enduring in affliction appears the most difficult. Fortunately, the other two make this one possible. If we rejoice in hope and persevere in prayer, we will be able to endure in suffering.

We rejoice in hope when we focus on hope, embrace hope, and determine to hope. To rejoice in hope is to regularly remind ourselves of the cause for our hope—the loving mercy of God. To rejoice in hope is to return again and again to the joyful message of salvation found in Scripture—the message that our God loves us so much that, although we were sinners, he became man, suffered, died, and rose so that we might be completely forgiven and that we might be able to share in the infinite joy he desires for us. To rejoice in hope is to constantly cry out in the words given to St. Faustina by our Lord, "Jesus, I trust in you!"

We persevere in prayer when we remain in constant dialogue with God. We must always talk to God, about anything and everything. We must share our concerns with God and ask him for help. We must tell God of our aspirations and ask for guidance. We must praise God for his glory and thank him for his countless gifts to us. We must laugh with God in times of joy, cry out to him in times of pain, and beg him in times of need. We persevere in prayer when we petition God even though we might doubt he is listening, and we persevere in prayer when we cry out to him even though we might doubt he exists.

To persevere in prayer when we doubt that our prayer is heard is the greatest act of prayer. Similarly, to rejoice in hope when we feel no hope is the greatest act of hope because "hope that sees for itself is not hope" (Rom 8:2). Rather, true hope is to hope when we do not see. Despite how daunting this appears, we can persevere in prayer and rejoice in hope, confident in God's love and mindful of his promise of salvation. God's love for us never ceases. He never abandons us. He never withdraws his offer of mercy.

God's consolation will only be withheld from us for a period of time. If we persevere, we will again feel his deep, abiding presence. How long we shall have to endure is never known to us, but God will not remain hidden for longer than we can bear. And it is in these times of apparent abandonment that we are actually the closest to God, for it is at these times that we most closely resemble Christ on the Cross.

We groan. At times, we groan more loudly than at others. But let us remain in hope, for one day all of our groaning will end. And when it does, we will receive the reward of our hope.

THREE

Old Testament Stories of Hope

Hope is the predominant theme of the Old Testament. In fact, it would be appropriate to refer to the Old Testament as the story of hope. The Old Testament is referred to as *salvation history* because it is the story of how God revealed to mankind his plan for their salvation—salvation *from* sin and death and salvation *for* glorification and eternal joy in Heaven through the salvific work of Jesus.

The Old Testament is a story of hopeful longing. Immediately after the Fall, God the Father began to reveal his plan to send his Son to save us. At first, he revealed his plan with only veiled references, for example, when he told Adam and Eve that the woman's offspring would strike the head of the serpent (the *protoevangelium*). Then God foreshadowed the coming of his Son in the lives of key biblical figures. Some examples include:

- **Abel,** the first man killed for being just;
- **Noah,** through whom a type of re-creation was effected;
- **Job,** who suffered unjustly to testify to the glory of God;
- **Melchizedek,** a priest of God with no beginning or end;

- **Abraham,** the trusting son of the Father from whom God's people sprung;
- **Joseph,** who suffered unjustly in order that he would be able to save those who caused his suffering;
- **Moses,** who mediated between man and God, and gave the Law;
- **Joshua,** who led his people into the Promised Land;
- **David,** a gentle shepherd who conquered all of his enemies; and
- **Jonah,** the voice of God who spent three days in the belly of the whale before being "resurrected" and saving the people.

God further revealed his plan through the words of the prophets. They predicted the coming of the Messiah who would save the people from their enemies. The prophets also hinted at the Messiah's unique nature, and foretold of the eternal salvation that would be accomplished through him.

By immersing ourselves in the Old Testament, we can come to feel the longing of the people for salvation. We can hear their groaning in the grip of sin and separation from God. We can experience the hope revealed by God and embraced by his faithful. It is as if all creation was on edge, buzzing with anticipation, when St. John the Baptist appeared and heralded the coming of Jesus.

We can greatly benefit from reflecting upon a few of the stories of hope contained in the Old Testament.

Abraham. Abraham is the quintessential personification of hope. He believed all God revealed to him. He trusted that

God's promises to him would be fulfilled. He did as he was asked by God. Of Abraham the *Catechism* says, "Hoping against hope, he believed, and thus became the father of many nations" (*CCC*, 1819; Rom 4:18).

It all started with an extraordinary request by God, "Go forth from your land, your relatives, and from your father's house to a land that I will show you. I will make of you a great nation, and I will bless you" (Gn 12:1–2). That was an awful lot for God to require of Abraham. He was asked to leave his land, his relatives, and his way of life. He was asked to leave a place that, according to archaeologists, was apparently a highly developed civilization, and head out into the desert to some yet unknown location. At age seventy-five, when Abraham found himself "very rich in cattle, in silver and in gold" (Gn 13:2), he was asked to throw out his retirement plans and head out into the unknown.

So what was Abraham's response? Was it, "You want me to do what? Lord who?" No, God's extraordinary request was met with an extraordinary response. Abraham gathered up his possessions and all the people attached to him, and left as the Lord asked. Abraham hoped in the Lord's words, and his hope was fulfilled. But Abraham exhibited even greater hope than this.

After years of wandering, Abraham called upon the Lord and reminded him that he and his wife still were without child. God promised that, despite Abraham and Sarah's advanced age, they would have innumerable descendants. Abraham responded to the Lord's promise with hope. He trusted that God would fulfill his promise (cf. Gn 15:1–6). And God did fulfill his promise: Sarah bore Abraham a son named Isaac, but not until Abraham was 100 years old.

We could stop at this point, and we would be amply impressed with both Abraham's hope and God's faithfulness. But, the story gets even better. At a later point,[1] God instructed Abraham to take Isaac with him up Mount Moriah and offer Isaac as a burnt sacrifice. These instructions sorely tested Abraham's hope. God had promised Abraham that he would have countless descendants, yet now God was asking him to kill his only son. Was God going to have Sarah bear Abraham another child when Abraham was now even more advanced in age? That must have seemed impossible to Abraham. Yet, God had fulfilled all of his other promises. So what was Abraham to do? He did as he had always done, he hoped in the Lord.

In response to God's request, Abraham set out the next day with Isaac. He took the wood for the burnt offering and laid it on the back of Isaac for him to carry. They went to the top of the mountain. Abraham built an altar, laid Isaac on it, and prepared to sacrifice him—when suddenly, the Lord stayed his hand (cf. Gn 22:1–19). And the Lord declared, "Because you acted as you did in not withholding from me your son, your only one, I will bless you and make your descendants as countless as the stars of the sky and the sands of the seashore; your descendants will take possession of the gates of their enemies, and in your descendants all the nations of the

---

[1] The Bible does not state clearly when this occurred, but Isaac was at least old enough to carry a large amount of wood. Some commentators suggest Isaac was as old as 25 or even 33.

earth will find blessing, because you obeyed my command" (Gn 22:16–18).

The hope of Abraham was such that he trusted in all God revealed. When he could not see the way, Abraham hoped that God would lead him. When he left his safety, Abraham hoped that God would protect him. When it appeared he would lose everything, Abraham hoped that God would provide all that he needed. When something seemed impossible, Abraham hoped that God would do the impossible. Abraham always hoped that God would somehow bring joy and blessing out of what appeared to be the most desperate and sorrowful future.

God brought all of Abraham's hope to fruition. He fulfilled all of his promises to Abraham. God blessed Abraham and made him a great nation. He gave Abraham descendants more countless than the sand of the seashore or the stars in the sky. In fact, from his descendants would come the Messiah and Savior of the world, Jesus Christ.

God so loved Abraham for his hope that he made of Abraham a representation of himself. He allowed Abraham to testify, by his life, to the mercy of God and the ultimate fulfillment of hope in God. Abraham was willing to give up his only son as God was willing to give up his. The wood that was placed on Isaac's back foreshadowed the wood of the Cross that was placed on the back of Jesus. But in his infinite mercy, God did not exact the life of Isaac, but instead gave that of his own beloved Son.

Moses. Moses was called to live in the hope of Heaven prefigured as the *Promised Land*—"a land flowing with milk and honey" (Ex 3:8). Moses was asked by God to return to Egypt (where he was wanted for murder) and demand that Pharaoh (one of the most powerful rulers in the world) release the Israelites (the Egyptians' slave labor force). Moses was then asked to lead the people across the wilderness (a path Moses had never traveled) to a land inhabited by numerous tribes (who would understandably be less than enthusiastic about the Israelites' taking over). Moses would also have to convince the Israelites that God sent him, and to do so he would have to overcome the fact that he wasn't much of a public speaker (perhaps he even suffered from a speech impediment). Despite the daunting task, like Abraham, Moses did what God asked.

The Bible provides us with a great deal of insight into the virtue of hope embraced by Moses. We learn of the people's constant rebellion against both God and Moses. We read of their continuous dissatisfaction with Moses's leadership and their distrust of God. We also learn about the daily challenges faced by Moses—governing the people, providing food and water, and defending the people from attacks of various tribes along the journey.

Moses was called to live in hope when he must have felt absolutely alone, at times, in his hope. Moses descended the mountain with the Ten Commandments to find his people had given up on him and God, reveling before a golden calf. No matter how miraculously God provided food and water, the people doubted God and even suggested that slavery in Egypt would be better than following God and his prophet Moses. Even when they arrived at the Promised Land, the elders convinced the people that, despite all of the miracles they had experienced (including the obliteration of Pharaoh's army), there was no way they could successfully defeat the inhabitants of the land. Even Aaron, Moses's right hand man, was disloyal to Moses and God at times.

With one exception, when Moses apparently doubted that God would send water from the rock, he hoped completely in God. He trusted God when things looked impossible, and remained hopeful that God would fulfill his promises and bring his people to their destination, even when he was apparently the only person who had such hope. And, despite all of their grumblings against him and their unfaithfulness to God, Moses continually hoped for the people, begging for God's forgiveness on their behalf.

Job. Job was not perfect, but he was certainly heroic in his hope. Though Job had shortcomings, through him we are able to learn the truth of hope. The story of Job is the story of perseverance in hope during times of incredible trial. Job assures us that no matter how intense the suffering and no matter how bleak things appear, God loves us. The pain will eventually end. We are destined for eternal joy. But Job does not sugarcoat reality. We will suffer. We will feel like all is lost. But we must still hope.

Job was a good and righteous man. He was filled with the virtue of hope. But, the devil wished to prove to God that Job was only filled with hope because God blessed Job with great prosperity. The devil bet God that Job would immediately abandon hope if his prosperity ended. Confident in Job, God allowed the devil to test Job.

The devil inflicted unimaginable suffering upon Job: Job lost his great wealth. His seven sons and three daughters died. His servants were murdered. He was afflicted with sores that covered his entire body. He was chastised by his wife. And he was ridiculed mercilessly by his friends.

Job would appear to have had every reason to abandon all hope in God. Job did not merely experience a lack of proof that God was concerned for him. Rather, Job had every reason to believe that God was personally punishing him. In fact, Job's friends went to extraordinary lengths to convince him that he had no reason for hope and was obviously accursed by God. Even his wife taunted him with the words, "Are you still holding to your innocence? Curse God and die" (Jb 2:9)!

But Job refused to abandon hope in God. He pointed out that as we gladly accept good from the hand of God, we must also accept the evil that God allows us to experience. In the depths of his suffering, Job refused to curse God as his wife proposed, but instead praised God. Tearing his garments and falling to the ground in worship, Job proclaimed, "The LORD gave and the LORD has taken away; blessed be the name of the LORD!"

There is one instance where Job fell short. While he accepted all that was happening to him, Job was very vocal in defending his innocence, claiming not to deserve the punishments he received. Job also questioned God as to why he allowed these things to happen. In response, God made his presence known to Job, but did not answer Job's question. Rather, God in effect said, "I am God, you are not, and that is enough for you right now." In response, Job repented for questioning God, praised him and acknowledged that God's ways were above his understanding. Job even petitioned God for mercy upon all his friends who wrongfully accused him. Then Job's hope was fulfilled. God returned him to health and prosperity, double what he had previously possessed. He had seven more sons and three more daughters, and he lived 140 years to see four generations of his children's children.

Hannah. Like Job, Hannah teaches us the virtue of hope in the midst of suffering. Her story assures us that God listens to our prayers and has our best interests in mind. In his dealings with Hannah, God reveals the great things that he can and will bring about unexpectedly.

Hannah was a woman of suffering. She greatly desired a child but was barren. As a result, she suffered the taunts of her husband's other wife who had born him many children. Despite her age and apparent infertility, Hannah never gave up hope in the Lord. Rather, she prayed constantly for a son.

Even in her great desire for a child, Hannah was not selfish but desired that the Lord's will, not hers, be done. Hannah promised that if she were to bear a son, she would give him to the Lord. Hannah's hope was finally rewarded, and she bore a son. For her part, Hannah remained faithful, giving her son Samuel into the service of the priest Eli.

Hannah's hope bore fruit not only for her but for all. Samuel grew up to be a holy and faithful servant of the Lord; he was both a great judge and a great prophet. God chose Samuel to anoint David as King of Israel, from whose line Christ would be born.

Ruth. Ruth is an unexpected example of the theological virtue of hope. She was not even a daughter of Israel but a Gentile. Yet, Ruth embraced the Lord and his people, trusting completely in God.

Naomi and her husband, Elimelech, left Bethlehem in a time of great famine to settle in Moab. There they had two sons who married two Moabite women, Ruth and Orpah. Elimelech and his two sons died, leaving the three women widows and destitute. Naomi realized that she had to return to her ancestral home, but also realized that there was little hope for her there and even less for her daughters-in-law. Naomi, therefore, advised the two women to return to their own families. Orpah took this advice, but Ruth begged Naomi to be allowed to return to Bethlehem with her: "Wherever you go I will go, wherever you lodge I will lodge. Your people shall be my people and your God, my God" (Ru 1:16).

Ruth returned to Bethlehem and submitted to the ways of the Israelites. She remained loyal to Naomi, providing for them by picking the remnants of grain left from the harvest. Having observed Ruth's devotion, a wealthy distant relative of Naomi named Boaz married Ruth, who became a full member of the Israelites. She bore a son who was the grandfather of King David. Thus God fulfilled Ruth's hope far beyond her expectations, choosing that his own Son, Jesus Christ, would be born of Ruth's line. At a time when sons were perceived to be of greater value than daughters, Ruth was praised as being "worth more than seven sons" (Ru 4:15)!

Judith. During the time of Judith, God's people were under attack by the Assyrians. They found themselves in the city of Bethulia, under siege by an army led by the general Holofernes. The situation was dire, and many despaired. Only a widow named Judith remained unshaken in her hope for God's deliverance.

Judith was a beautiful and capable woman. After the death of her husband, she managed her fields, livestock, servants, and maids. She was devout and fasted regularly. Judith was respected by all and "no one had a bad word to say about her, for she feared God greatly" (Jdt 8:8).

As famine began to spread over the besieged city, the people lost hope that God would deliver them, and so they contemplated surrendering. In fact, the elders and people decided to put an ultimatum upon God—he must deliver them within five days or they would surrender. In response, Judith gathered the elders and reprimanded them for their lack of hope. She chastised them for their arrogance of putting God to the test. Judith was rock solid in her hope and trusted completely in God's will, stating, "So while we wait for the salvation that comes from him, let us call upon him to help us, and he will hear our cry if it pleases him" (Jdt 8:18). Judith even urged the elders to thank God for putting their hope to the test with the dire conditions.

Judith exhibited true hope. In the midst of almost certain defeat by the enemy, Judith trusted God completely. She trusted that whatever the outcome, it would be the will of God. She prayed to God for deliverance in complete hope: "Your strength is not in numbers, nor does your might depend upon the powerful. You are God of the lowly, helper of those of little account, supporter of the weak, protector of those in despair, savior of those without hope" (Jdt 9:11).

God heard Judith's prayer and granted deliverance to his people through her hand. God blessed her and enabled her to infiltrate the camp of the enemy and gain the favor of Holofernes. While Holofernes lay in a drunken stupor, Judith cut off his head with his own sword. She returned to her people with the head and rallied them to attack the Assyrians. Having lost their leader, the Assyrians were dispirited, and were thus easily routed by the Israelites. Judith was praised with the words, "Your deed of hope will never be forgotten by those who recall the might of God" (Jdt 13:19).

FOUR

Jesus Christ Our Reason for Hope

Words of Hope

"Take heart! I have overcome the world" (Jn 16:33, NIV). Just before Jesus submitted to his Passion and Death, he sought to prepare his disciples for what was to come. Jesus knew that their hope would be put to the test. The disciples would witness the religious and political leaders of their society turn on Jesus, condemn him, torture him, and put him to death. Jesus assured them his Death would not be the end and hinted, once again, to his Resurrection: "A little while and you will no longer see me, and again a little while later and you will see me" (Jn 16:16). But Jesus sought to strengthen them (and us) far beyond the Resurrection.

Jesus was aware his Death was only the beginning of the trials that his followers would experience. After Jesus rose from the dead and appeared to the disciples, he would ascend to Heaven. And then the real trials would begin for them. At that point, each of the Apostles, except Judas, would be challenged to live constantly in hope as they went "out to all the earth" (Rom 10:18) to share the Gospel. Each of them would meet great resistance.

Each of them would share deeply in the sufferings of Christ. And every one of them, save St. John, would be martyred.

At the same time that Jesus warned the Apostles that they would suffer, he offered them great hope. He acknowledged that the world would hate them but reminded them that in receiving the world's hate, they were united to him: "If the world hates you, realize that it hated me first" (Jn 15:18). And, Jesus assured them that the hatred of the world was of no importance and no hindrance to their hope, for he had conquered the world!

The world could neither tempt Jesus with its false promises nor sway him from his obedience to the Father's will. The world could neither silence Jesus's message nor thwart his plan. No amount of humiliation, pain, or even death could stop Jesus from accomplishing his salvific work. Instead, in submitting to those things, his saving work was perfected. Jesus humbled himself before the opposition of the world and submitted himself to death as a sacrifice for us. But in taking his life, the world did not win. Jesus rose from the dead, thus obliterating death and opening the gates of eternal life for all who would follow him.

The Apostles took heart and persisted in overcoming the world in Christ's name. They witnessed to the Good News of salvation through both their testimony and their lives. While all but St. John abandoned Jesus at the time of his death, they all found the courage to give their own lives for him. Empowered by the Holy Spirit, a handful of nobodies from nowhere ignited a spark of faith that set the world on fire, and that fire continues to burn today.

We, too, must take heart. The world that hated Jesus and hated his Apostles is the same world that hates us today. It is the world of selfishness and indifference. It is the world of relativism and intolerance. It is the world that is scared of us because we are different. We are in the world, but not of the world. We are merely passing through this world. Our hope is set on the world that is to come. Like the Apostles, the examples of our lives are a challenge to the world. We are the light of truth that illuminates the darkness of ignorance and sin.

Sometimes we may feel like we are alone. In such times, we must rejoice in hope. In such times, we must resemble Christ. And we must never despair. We must never lose hope. We must take heart, for Christ has already won. He has conquered the world and obtained Heaven for us!

"A little while and you will no longer see me, and again a little while later and you will see me" (Jn 16:16). Before his Passion and Death, Jesus used these words to encourage his disciples. But, these words perplexed them. They asked each other, "What is this 'little while' [of which he speaks]? We do not know what he means" (Jn 16:18). So Jesus continued, "Amen, amen, I say to you, you will weep and mourn, while the world rejoices; you will grieve, but your grief will become joy … So you also are now in anguish. But I will see you again, and your hearts will rejoice, and no one will take your joy away from you" (Jn 16:20–22).

These words of Jesus were meant to be somewhat mysterious; their import could not be fully understood by the disciples at the time. In fact, these words of hope were not meant solely for those disciples, but were also meant for all who hear them today.

The immediate significance of these words was a warning to Jesus's disciples concerning his impending Passion and Death, but these words also offered them hope because of his promise to return. In a little while the disciples would no longer see Jesus. First, they would no longer see him because he would be dragged away by the temple guard. They would also no longer see him at that point because they would run away. A little more in the future, the disciples would no longer see him because Jesus would die. But Jesus assured them that this would not be the end, promising that they would see him again soon. He would rise from the dead and appear to them.

Jesus's words also foretold what would happen after his Resurrection and even what would happen after that. After his Resurrection he would eventually leave his disciples again to ascend to the Father. After his Ascension, he would see them once more at their own death and resurrection. At that point, they would never be separated from him again, and Jesus's words of hope would be fulfilled: "Your hearts will rejoice, and no one will take your joy away from you" (Jn 16:22).

The biggest challenge for the disciples to remain in hope came after Jesus left them at his Ascension and passed on his mission to them. It was then that the disciples became responsible for continuing the work Jesus had started; they were responsible for spreading the truth of Jesus, starting with the very people who denied him and put him to death. Although they were extremely successful, their success came with great personal sacrifice. The disciples encountered ridicule from their own people, family, and leaders. They were opposed by all the people to whom they preached the Good News—Romans and Greeks, Gentiles and Jews alike. Many disciples were tried in Jewish courts, imprisoned, whipped, and put to death. Some were stoned, hung, crucified, dragged by horses, and thrown off a building, while others were clubbed, beheaded, flogged, and shot with arrows. But hope saw them through all these terrible tortures and deaths. Even at the most gruesome and desperate of times, they trusted in the words of Jesus; that in a little while, they would see him again, never to be separated again.

Jesus's words were also spoken to us. Sometimes we can see Jesus or feel his presence in the youthful exuberance of receiving him in First Holy Communion, in the consolation felt at the funeral of a family member, in the answer of prayer for one in great need, in the life of a saintly person, in the eyes of a newborn child or grandchild, in random moments in Mass, or in prayer when we feel his warm embrace. At other times, Jesus might seem hidden—during our adolescence when we attended Mass with our family out of obligation rather than desire; when we are heartbroken at the loss of a parent, spouse, or child; during an illness that lingered without relief; at the loss of a job; at the time of a divorce; or when we looked at the world and felt like it was becoming increasingly evil. At these times, when we cannot see him, Jesus speaks directly to us. We will see him again in a little while. The pain will end. The consolation will come. Jesus asks us to never give up hope, but to always look for him—in prayer, in the Tabernacle, in the Eucharist, in the confessional, and in our brothers and sisters. And Jesus assures us that in a little while in Heaven our hearts will rejoice and we will never be separated from him ever again.

"Ask and it will be given to you; seek and you will find; knock and the door will be opened to you" (Mt 7:7). We have heard this verse from Scripture so many times that perhaps it has lost meaning. If so, it is time for us to revisit this verse and look at it, as if for the first time, because it is one of the most powerful and hopeful passages in all of Scripture.

Jesus is not speaking in a veiled or metaphoric style. Rather, he clearly and directly states, "Ask and it will be given to you; seek and you will find; knock and the door will be opened to you." Lest there be any question what he meant, Jesus immediately follows this statement with, "For everyone who asks, receives; and the one who seeks, finds; and to the one who knocks, the door will be opened" (Mt 7:8). But Jesus didn't stop there. He hammered home the point, further expanding what he meant: "Which one of you would hand his son a stone when he asks for a loaf of bread, or a snake when he asks for a fish? If you then, who are wicked, know how to give good gifts to your children, how much more will your heavenly Father give good things to those who ask him" (Mt 7:9–11).

Jesus was not a liar. He would never mislead us or deceive us. Jesus promises that if we seek him, we will find him. Maybe not this very moment and maybe not even tomorrow, but we will find him at some point. And when we do find Jesus, though we might not find him exactly as we had envisioned him, we will find him as he truly is—something, no, someone far beyond anything we could have ever imagined.

If we ask, we will receive. What will we receive? That which is best for us. God is not merely a better version of a good parent, but the archetype of a loving parent. He wants to give us every good thing, never giving us bad when we ask for good. Nor will he give us bad, though we might mistakenly ask for it. Even if we ask for the ultimate bad—eternal separation from him in Hell—he will give us uncountable chances to change our mind. In fact, God never truly gives us Hell; we give it to ourselves when we do not choose God.

If we knock on his door, he *will* open it to us. We can choose not to knock and not to enter Heaven, but Heaven remains completely accessible to us. Jesus assures us that if we truly desire Heaven, Heaven will be ours. This is our true reason for hope. No matter what we experience, no matter what pain or doubt we feel here on earth—our eternal joy is assured if we truly desire it.

"Let not your heart be troubled" (Jn 14:1, emphasis added). So many of Jesus's words of hope were, like these, spoken to his Apostles just before his Passion. Ignoring his impending Passion and Death, Jesus reached out to console and strengthen his followers. Jesus knew the trials they would undergo. He was aware of the fear and doubt they would experience. In spite of this, or rather because of this, Jesus admonished them not to let their hearts be troubled.

Jesus assured his disciples that he was going ahead of them. He would pave the way for them to follow. He would prepare a room for them in his Father's house. He would return. And he would then take them with him so that where he was, they might also be (cf. Jn 14:2–3).

Jesus makes the same promise to each of us. He has walked the path here on earth that we must walk. He has experienced the pain and suffering that we will experience. He faced the fears that we face. He submitted to death, which we too must experience. But we will experience none of these things alone. Rather, Jesus will be with us through all of them. And, Jesus assures us that he has opened the doors to Heaven and will lead us through them to life eternal.

Our hearts are, unfortunately, often troubled. We often feel lost and scared. We ask the same question the Apostle Thomas put to Jesus, "How can we know the way" (Jn 14:5)? Jesus quiets our doubts, saying, "I am the way and the truth and the life" (Jn 14:6).

Jesus is the way. When we are lost, we need merely look at him and follow the way he leads. Jesus is the truth. When we do not know the answer or when we question ourselves or the world around us, we need merely listen to Jesus's words and follow his example. Jesus is the life. His words are the words of everlasting life. In Jesus, we are assured of life—life in abundance; life not merely for twenty or fifty or even one hundred years, but for eternity.

"Let your hearts not be troubled" is not the same as "you will never be troubled." It is not a promise but an admonition. Jesus challenges us to increase in hope, and so we must fight against despair. We must constantly remind ourselves that God loves us so much that he suffered, died, and rose for us so that we might be forever joyful with him one day. If we desire that our hearts not be troubled, we must focus on Jesus rather than ourselves, especially in the times when our hope wavers. To "let not our hearts be troubled" means to cry out again and again through tears of fear and sadness, "Jesus, I trust in You!"

"Let not your heart be troubled" is also an assurance. Jesus assures us that there really is no reason for our hearts to be troubled. He has gone before us and prepared the way. He is also always with us, despite what we *feel* at any given moment. Jesus has overcome the world. He has paved the way to himself. He has prepared a place for us in Heaven. He stands waiting at the door. We need merely seek, ask, and knock.

Example of Hope

Jesus did not merely preach hope. He lived it. Being fully human, Jesus was subject to the same challenges as us. He was tempted to abandon hope, but he never did. Therefore, Jesus is the perfect example of hope. As such, we must learn from his example and imitate him as closely as possible. Jesus is also the perfect source of hope. Being fully human, Jesus is aware of our struggle to remain in hope, and, being fully God, he is able to assist us in that struggle. Let us then reflect upon some examples of hope that Jesus gave us, knowing he will help us as we seek to walk in his ways.

Conforming his will to that of the Father. Obeying the will of God is perhaps the most perfect expression of hope; it is an act of complete trust in God. By conforming our will to God's will, we trust that he knows better what is good for us than we do. By conforming our will to God's will, we trust that he will take care of everything in the best possible way. The *virtue* of hope is expressed in the fact that God wills what is perfectly and eternally good for us. The *act* of hope is expressed in our trust in God.

Though Jesus was God, he was also man. As man, Jesus was prone to the weakness of mankind. He was tempted to place his human desires above those of God. This is poignantly seen in the devil's temptation of Jesus. The devil tempted him with desires of the body, the eyes, and the ego, but Jesus gave into none of them (cf. Mt 4:1–11). Jesus's rejection of those desires demonstrates that none of them can truly satisfy man. Rather, God alone is the source of man's satisfaction.

As man, Jesus practiced hope by conforming his human will to the divine will—the will of his Father. Jesus said to the people, "I came down from heaven not to do my own will but the will of the one who sent me" (Jn 6:38). In fact, Jesus completely subjugated his human will to that of God's, stating, "I do nothing on my own, but I say only what the Father taught me...I always do what is pleasing to him" (Jn 8:28–29). For Jesus, no human desire, even a bodily need, was more important than the desire to do the will of the Father, which is all-sustaining: "My food is to do the will of the one who sent me and to finish his work" (Jn 4:34).

We see the conflict between the natural and heavenly will in Jesus's Agony in the Garden. Although Jesus was aware of his impending arrest, torture, and death, he did not run away. Instead, he went to a place to pray and prepare himself. In this place, Jesus confronted his natural human desire for self-preservation. Jesus prayed that, if it were possible, he might not endure the suffering ahead of him, but he also prayed, at the same time, that God's will be done.

Jesus petitioned his Father three times in what is the perfect example of how we should petition God. We should lay our desires before the Father, while, at the same time, desiring God's will be done—even if his will contradicts our will. Jesus first requested to be spared from undergoing his Passion and Death, unless his Father desired it of him, praying, "My Father, if it is possible, let this cup pass from me; yet, not as I will, but as you will" (Mt 26:39). Then, as Jesus began to discern that the Father willed him to undergo the Passion, Jesus assured the Father of his assent to the Father's will, praying, "My Father, if it is not possible that this cup pass without my drinking it, your will be done!" Then he prayed a third time, saying the same thing, resigning himself completely to the will of the Father.

As a human, Jesus did not want to suffer and die. As a human, Jesus must have been terrified by the kind of torture and death he would soon experience. Also as a human, Jesus was able to exercise his free will and place the needs of all mankind over his own personal human needs. As the perfect human, Jesus conformed his own will perfectly to the will of his Heavenly Father. Jesus lived in perfect hope, understanding that his Passion and Death, despite its repugnance, was absolutely necessary for the salvation of mankind.

We are to follow the example of Christ as best we can. We are called to hope in the will of the Father. We are to trust that God's will is best for us, even when his will seems in direct contradiction to what we perceive as best for us.

Trusting in the Apostles. Hope requires us to trust in that which does not necessarily, in outward appearance, seem trustworthy. It is the acceptance that God can and will accomplish his goals through unlikely means. Hope requires us to recognize that (1) we often don't know exactly how God desires his will to unfold and (2) it is often not up to us to accomplish God's will in a particular situation.

It is ironic that Jesus—Almighty God, Lord of lords and master of the universe—was the antithesis of a control freak. Jesus lived with complete trust; he even trusted those who did not earn his trust. And this is because Jesus trusted that the will of his Father would be accomplished through very ordinary human beings.

Jesus spent only approximately three years in public ministry. After accomplishing his work of salvation—suffering, dying, and rising from the dead—Jesus remained with his disciples for only forty days and then left, trusting the dissemination of everything he said and did to a handful of followers. This trust sounds unbelievable, and is even more so when we consider the men to whom he entrusted his mission of salvation. Some might even characterize it as disconcerting.

None of the Apostles had particularly impressive credentials. They were not, for the most part, learned men. Many were fishermen. None of them were priests or leaders of the people. Yet Jesus chose each of them personally. And, when he left, Jesus entrusted the entire world into their care.

From a human perspective, the Apostles did not act, in the three years they spent with Jesus, in a way that would engender confidence. They argued as to who was the greatest (cf. Mk 9:33). They made power plays for the best positions in Heaven (cf. Mk 10:35–37). They tried to convince Jesus not to carry out his mission (cf. Mt 16:21–23). They failed to stay awake during his agony in the garden (cf. Mk 14:32–37). They deserted Jesus when he was arrested (cf. Mt 26:56). They swore they didn't even know him (cf. Mt 26:69–75). And even after Jesus rose and appeared to them, there was one Apostle, not present at Jesus's appearance, who refused to believe until he had put his fingers into the nail holes of Jesus's hands (cf. Jn 20:24–25).

Jesus hoped. He trusted that his work would not be in vain. He trusted that the Father's will would be accomplished. He trusted that these men, whom the Father had given to him, would not fail in their efforts to make known his saving work throughout the world and care for his Church. We now see that Jesus's trust in his disciples was well placed. They lived in hope and accomplished the tasks Jesus gave to them. Jesus has the same trust in each of us. We must in turn place our hope in him.

Before his hour of glory, Jesus made one final prayer of hope for those to whom he would task with carrying on his mission. This prayer is as much for us as it was for his original disciples.

> Holy Father, keep them in your name that you have given me, so that they may be one just as we are. When I was with them I protected them in your name that you gave me, and I guarded them.... I do not ask that you take them out of the world but that you keep them from the evil one.... As you sent me into the world, so I sent them into the world.... I pray not only for them, but also for those who will believe in me through their word, so that they may all be one, as you, Father, are in me and I in you, that they also may be in us, that the world may believe that you sent me. (Jn 17:11–21)

Surrendering to death. The ultimate example of hope by Jesus was surrendering to death. By nature, Jesus did not need to die. Even though he was human, like Adam and Eve, Jesus's human nature was not tainted with the stain of Original Sin; it was not subject to corruption. But Jesus desired to suffer death for our salvation, so he freely submitted to death.

Jesus is unique in his surrender to death. Adam and Eve originally would not have died, but because of sin they were forced to die. Many martyrs have chosen to accept death rather than prolong their lives, but they all would have ultimately experienced death. Jesus alone would never have had to die. In surrendering to death, Jesus demonstrated hope for all of us. He, who needed not die, chose to die so that we, who must die, might have hope of eternal life.

Because Jesus was fully human, it was natural for him to fear death. Yet, he, who could have avoided death, chose to die because he hoped perfectly. In his human nature, Jesus trusted that death would not be the end; he trusted that he would rise from the dead. Jesus not only died as a sacrifice for our sins, but also died in order to be an example of hope for us—to show all of us that death is not the end, but a new and eternal beginning.

We hope, in spite of death, because Jesus rose from the dead. Jesus alone has died and, of his own power, risen never to die again. There is no tomb on earth that holds the body of Jesus of Nazareth. We also hope because Jesus, who has complete power over death, assured us that death is not the end; instead, it is the beginning. We are invited to live in eternal joy with him in Heaven. We have hope because Jesus has given us cause for hope.

The Resurrection imparted hope to the disciples. Those who abandoned and denied Jesus changed completely because of the Resurrection. They subjected themselves to abuse, torture, and death in his name. Their natures, however, were not changed. They still possessed a natural fear of suffering and death. But, filled with hope, they overcame their fear and lovingly accepted death.

The hope of the disciples should also give us great hope. It is incredible to believe that a person would be willing to suffer and die for something he knew to be a complete lie. It is incredible that ten of the Apostles and countless other disciples would suffer and die for a complete lie. Through their example of hope, we have every reason to hope as well.

The Cross of Hope

Members of other Christian denominations often ask Catholics why the crucifix is such a predominant part of their religious tradition. As we mentioned briefly in our discussion of mercy, the crucifix is displayed prominently in Catholic churches, found on altars, hung on the walls of houses, and worn around people's necks. Some who are not used to this tradition feel as if it improperly emphasizes Christ's Death over his Resurrection—that it emphasizes the despair of Christ's Passion over the hope in his Resurrection, or that it is downright gloomy or even morbid. Nothing could be further from the truth. The Cross, not the Resurrection, is the true symbol of hope. The Cross testifies to the hope exhibited by Christ. And the Resurrection proves that Christ's hope on the Cross was well founded. At the Resurrection, in fact, there was no more need for hope. Christ had risen. Death was conquered. Hope had been fulfilled.

We embrace the Cross in our daily lives because of our great need of hope. As we suffer here on earth, separated from the full communion with God that we will enjoy in Heaven, we are called to persevere in hope. We look to the Cross for hope. We recognize the greatness of the Cross that our Lord carried successfully for us in comparison to the little crosses we carry, and are mindful that, for Christ, the Cross was not the end but a new eternal beginning.

When we, like Christ, have been raised, we will have no more need for hope. Our hope will be fulfilled. We will be united for all eternity with God. In Heaven, we will not focus on the moment of our resurrection because the eternal experience of perfect joy will exceed any moment of triumph. In Heaven, we will, however, be ever mindful of the Cross of Christ, which will not cause us sadness or remorse but great joy, because we will see the triumph of Jesus from which all joy flows.

We know from the Scripture accounts of Jesus's post-Resurrection appearances that the resurrected body of Christ was not constricted by time or space, nor did it necessarily take the form of Christ's body before death. How telling, then, is the fact that Christ's resurrected appearance would include the marks of the Cross (cf. Lk 24:39; Jn 20:27).

Evil desired the Cross to be the mechanism for death. Instead, it is the means to life. Evil desired the Cross to bring inconsolable pain. Instead, it brings eternal, unfathomable joy. Evil sought the Cross to be a sign of defeat and despair. Instead, it stands forever as the symbol of triumph and hope.

FIVE

Hope in Our Judgment

Each man receives his eternal retribution in his
immortal soul at the very moment of his death, in a
particular judgment that refers his life to Christ: either
entrance into the blessedness of heaven—through
a purification or immediately—or immediate
and everlasting damnation. (*CCC*, 1022)

Death brings an end to human life and an end to our time
for choosing between accepting and rejecting the salvation
offered through Jesus Christ. At our death, we will come
before the throne of God and be judged. The state of our soul
at that moment will decide what happens next.

If, during our lives, we have chosen to unite ourselves
with God to such an extent that we stand before the throne
in perfect purity, completely desirous, and ready to be
with him, we shall be immediately received into Heaven.
If we have generally chosen to unite ourselves with God,
but are not fully prepared for complete and perfect union
with him because of sin, we will be purified and prepared
fully through purgation before entering the Kingdom of

Heaven. If, however, in life we have chosen ourselves in preference to God and died without turning back to him, we will be given exactly what we chose—eternity in Hell, separated from God and all that is of God.

Often we fear God's Judgment, but hope assures us that such fear is misplaced. Our judgment is a source for immense joy and should be longed for.

Destined for Glory

Once again, we must return to where we started in our discussion of hope: hope as the theological virtue by which we desire Heaven *and trust that we will obtain Heaven.*

As we walk through life, we are innately aware that something is wrong. We are not complete. If we take a moment to truly examine the world around us, we will recognize that we don't quite *fit in.* We sense purpose to our existence but can't find anything here on earth that perfectly fulfills that sense of purpose. This is because we are destined for something else.

When we look deep into ourselves, we are aware that there is something that is not merely physical, something that pervades every element of our physicality. We are aware of a *me* that is united with our physical movement, but is not merely our physical movement. We are aware of a *me* that is united to our thoughts, but is not merely our thoughts. We are aware that we have a soul. Further, while we have a sense that our soul was created at some point, there is no logic to convince us that our soul comes to an end. Death is an enigma to us because we are innately aware of our immortality. We know that death is not the end and that there is nothing here on earth that fulfills our destiny. Therefore, we must be destined for something beyond the grave.

We are certainly not destined for Hell. We have been created beautifully by God. Through veiled references in the Old Testament and specific promises by Jesus, God has assured us that he wants us to live in perfect joy and unity with him, for all eternity. Time and time again, we turned our backs on God, but in his mercy, he always invited us to return to him. God sent patriarchs and prophets to prepare us for his only Son, whom he sent to die for us. He sent the Holy Spirit to be our guide, consoler, and advocate. He gave us the Sacraments. God has made it perfectly clear that we are not destined for Hell, but for Heaven.

At the end of time, after all people have been judged, the world shall be recreated, and we shall inhabit it in our resurrected bodies. Man is body and soul here on earth and will be body and soul in Heaven. But, our bodies shall be glorified. Our bodies shall no longer suffer sickness, corruption, death, or the physical limitations to which they are now subject. Our bodies will be radiant and beautiful and will express the purified nature of our soul. Our bodies will share in the perfection of the resurrected Body of Christ.

Hope is not a futile attempt at consolation for an inevitable oblivion. Rather, it is an assurance of the truth of our present and future. Hope reveals that we were made by God and for God, and that we will one day be with God for all eternity. We are not made for the grave; we are destined for glory!

Judge Me, Please!

We fear Judgment Day because we are afraid of its outcome. We are afraid of Hell. We fear our judgment because we see it as the vehicle by which we might be banished to eternal damnation. This fear is misplaced.

Objectively, it is understandable and perhaps appropriate to fear Hell. It is understandable to fear Hell because Hell is a thoroughly undesirable place, a place we never want to experience. Sometimes, focusing on the terror of Hell motivates us to avoid Hell and attain Heaven. But, the fear of Hell is not necessary for the soul that embraces the virtue of hope.

If we live in hope, there is no reason to fear Hell. For the soul that willingly receives God's grace and embraces a loving relationship with God, Hell is not a possible outcome. Hope is the *realistic expectation of Heaven* and the assured avoidance of Hell. This is not to say that Hell is not real. Jesus made it clear that there is a Hell and that souls will end up there, including some who outwardly appear to be his followers: "Not everyone who says to me, 'Lord, Lord,' will enter the kingdom of heaven" (Mt 7:21). But, *we* need not fear Hell.

Each of us is given the gift of hope and invited to respond in hope. We are invited to live in such a way that we need never fear Hell. God offers his love and allows us to respond in love. God has given us Christ as our Savior and invited us to accept the salvation won by him. God has given us the Law, the prophets, the Church, and the Bible so that we might always hear God and know the way to him. He has given us the Sacraments so that we might be fed regularly with grace—his own divine life living within us. God even gave us the Sacrament of Reconciliation, through which we can be assured of complete forgiveness by God of all sins we have committed. And let us never forget: God is mercy! He desires to shower his mercy upon us. If we ask for his mercy, we will receive it.

For the soul that lives in hope, there is only one possible outcome of God's judgment that is less than perfect. It is possible that while we might have embraced hope, we have not done so perfectly. Therefore, at the time of our death, there remains an impediment in our souls that stands in the way of complete union with God. In that case, we shall experience Purgatory. Is their pain in purgation? Yes, it's the pain of seeing God's glory fully revealed, possessing an absolute desire to be united with God and being denied that unity through one's own fault. But in Purgatory, the soul suffers joyfully, absolutely assured of its impending union with God.

We are destined for the glory of the resurrection. In hope, our judgment is not something to be feared but longed for. Judgment is necessary. It is the sure entryway to Heaven. Our attitude should always be, "Judge me, please!"

The Hope That Won't Disappoint

Maybe you dreamed for months of getting that awesome game for Christmas, only to be bored by it after playing it for a few minutes; maybe it was your first dance, and your date, the hunky jock, turned out to be a total jerk; maybe it was a bad interview or a dream house that turned into a complete nightmare. We have all looked forward to many things in our lives only to be very disappointed when we obtained them. But we must be careful not to let these earthly disappointments diminish the hope we have in God and in his promise of Heaven.

If we were honest, some of us would admit that we are a little fearful of Heaven. For some, pondering eternity feels like looking down from the Eiffel Tower when you have a fear of heights. Others have the hardest time conceiving even the smallest notion of what perfect happiness could be like. Still others just avoid thinking about Heaven because they are discomforted by anything they don't feel they can control. And some people are just generally afraid of the unknown. But hope assures us that despite these very human emotions, Heaven is not to be feared.

There is no reason to fear Heaven. St. Paul assures us that our hope in God and in Heaven is a hope that does not disappoint. It is a hope born of the love of God, which has been poured out into our hearts. It is a hope sustained by the Holy Spirit dwelling within us (cf. Rom 5:5). Hope is a gift given to us by our perfect, loving God and sustained in us by our perfect, loving God, and hope will lead us to our perfect, loving God.

God loves us perfectly and personally. He created us for Heaven. Therefore, it is ludicrous to think that Heaven will be anything but exactly what we desire. God alone knows what would fill us with perfect joy, and he alone can provide us with that perfect joy.

In Heaven, every fear will be banished and every tear wiped away. No pain, for any wrong committed by us or wrong done to us, will remain. Any brokenness within us will be mended, and anything lacking within us will be provided. In Heaven, we will be in true, complete, perfect union with God, our brothers and sisters, the angels, and all creation, while also retaining our individuality. In Heaven we will experience the absolute love of God and be able to love God absolutely in return. Heaven will bring us true and lasting peace, and, at the same time, thrilling ecstasy. In Heaven we will experience perfect, eternal joy.

SIX

The Practice of Hope

We began our discussion of hope by identifying the fact that hope is a virtue, a feeling, and an act. The theological virtue of hope has been infused into our souls and remains with us. The feeling of hope can come and go. It is our daily decision whether we will act in hope.

The practice of hope that we will address in this chapter concerns our ongoing efforts to act in hope, even when we might not *feel* hopeful. The practice of hope is first and foremost an act of the will; it is a decision to hope, regardless of whether or not we feel hope. Hope is also an act of the intellect. We must return again and again to Scripture, to the teachings and Tradition of the Church, and to the lives and advice of saints and other spiritual mentors in order to assure ourselves of the truth of hope.

The practice of hope can sometimes consist of a physical act. We might attend Mass, sit before the Tabernacle, kneel before the exposed Host, visit a pilgrimage site, verbalize some prayer, or maybe even just whisper the words, "Jesus, I trust in you!"—even when we feel no consolation while doing these things. The practice of hope often requires us to work toward steering our emotions so they are in conformity with the truth of hope. Sometimes we will need to let go of some fear or sadness. Other times we will merely need to redirect our tears toward the true cause of our sadness.

If we want to be better at our jobs, faster runners, or better pianists, we have to work at it. The same is true for hope. We need to work at hope if we want to increase in hope.

Keep Your Eye on the Prize

Anyone who has succumbed to the disease commonly referred to as golfing understands the sheer terror of the *water hole.* The afflicted person stands in the tee box and looks out over a seemingly endless expanse of water that is situated between the tee and the green. As the patient lines up his shot in the direction of the flag, his last feverish thought as he draws back the club is, "Please let me carry the water." The club mightily comes down and *tops* the ball, sending it straight into the hazard, where it sinks to its watery grave.

The golfer did not miss his mark. In fact, the ball went exactly where he aimed it. His failure was to lose sight of the target. In his fear, the golfer focused not on the flag, but on the water. And that's exactly where the ball ended up. The best advice for this golfer (short of giving up golf) is simple: ignore the water and focus on the flag. We should pay heed to the same advice when it comes to practicing hope in order to maintain undistracted focus.

The first step to practicing of hope is identifying the proper object of our hope. That object should be apparent by now— God. He is the source of our hope because hope comes from him. He created us and infused the virtue of hope in us. We did not earn hope. Rather, God freely gave it to us. Even our acts of hope are nothing more than a response to God's initial act of hope.

God is the goal of our hope. As we have acknowledged many times, in many ways, we were made by God, for God. We are aimed toward God because we want to be with God, in Heaven, for all eternity.

God is the reason for our hope. If there is no God, there is no hope. Life without God would be a meaningless exercise in futility in which we enjoyed momentary lapses of pleasure to break our otherwise monotonous and miserable lives.

God is the strength for our hope. God pours out the Holy Spirit into our souls to guide us, and he gives us sacramental grace to fortify us. When we cry out to God in our weakness, he carries us in hope.

Having identified God as the object of our hope, we can move onto the second step in the practice of hope—how to focus on that object. While the need to focus on God, as the object of our hope, might seem obvious, it is actually quite challenging. We are distracted by the world and tempted by our egos.

The world around us can be very distracting to the practice of hope. First, there is tragedy. We see so much pain and suffering in the world—wars, natural disasters, starvation, sickness, disease, corruption, betrayal, etc. These evils can quickly drag our spirits down into despair. The news media seems determined to make us focus on nothing but the bad in the world. Based solely on the ratio of bad news to good news reported, one might believe that there is almost no good in the world. This misinformed, false conclusion can even lead some people to believe the age-old lie that a good God would never allow such evil.

Even good, practicing Christians can sometimes be distracted from God, as the source of hope, by the evil in the world. We can become overly focused on evils such as legalized abortion, pornography, unjust political structures, and poverty. While it is good to recognize these evils and good to take action against them, we must never become so focused on them that we lose focus on God. God is aware of these evils and far more saddened by them than are we. Yet, he allows them to happen in order that a greater good might come about (though we might not be able to comprehend all, a fraction, or any of that good). We must bring God into all of our efforts to combat these evils. While we are making practical efforts to alleviate suffering, we must also pray, look for the face of God in the oppressed, bring the love of Christ to them, and speak the truth in love (even to politicians who oppose God's good). We must take care that our efforts are not mere *social activism*, but corporal and spiritual works of mercy.

Jesus reminded us that the poor will always be with us. During the life of Jesus, when God walked the earth as man, evil was still present. Yet, Jesus required only one thing—that people focus on him. Martha was indignant that her sister Mary—who just sat at Jesus's feet, listening to him—wouldn't help her with the unpleasant chores of hosting a guest, and one so special as Jesus. Martha requested that Jesus should make Mary help her. But the response Jesus gave to her request was not the one she expected. Jesus said, "Martha, Martha, you are anxious and worried about many things. There is need of only one thing. Mary has chosen the better part and it will not be taken from her" (Lk 10:41–42).

We can also become distracted by the world when things are going well. Health and prosperity can lessen our need of hope, sometimes to the point where we feel that we don't really need God. But, God is the source of all the good that we experience. And even the best of goods in this world are mere reflections of the good that awaits us in Heaven. Also, the good times never last. We can never outrun calamities; sickness and death will ultimately find us all. And when they come, we will be hard-pressed to return to that long-abandoned hope.

Our egos can also lead us away from hope. We can easily fall into a false belief that we can *do it on our own*. Often, we can come to believe that we are the authors of our own destiny, whether that be in good or bad times. In troubling times, we might attribute our perseverance through them to our own fighting spirit. In good times, we might attribute our success solely to our own efforts.

God is both the source of and the reason for hope. Therefore, if we wish to live in hope, we must focus on God, not on our self. If we rely on our own strength in trying to practice hope, sooner or later we will fail and then fall into despair. Despite whether things are going well or poorly, we must ask God to fill us with and sustain us in hope. In the words of a great Catholic author, Fr. Leo Trese, "A saint might be described as one who has the utmost distrust of his own strength, and the utmost confidence in God."[1]

Endure, Persevere, and Rejoice

St. Paul provides us with a formula for the practice of hope. He urges us to endure suffering patiently, persevere in prayer, and rejoice in hope (cf. Rom 12:12). He reminds us that suffering is inevitable and that no one can avoid it entirely. But, we can all choose how we will react to suffering. Suffering can challenge our hope, but it need not negate our hope. In fact, it can be a means by which our hope is deepened.

As we have already discussed, suffering is generally not a punishment from God, nor is the existence of suffering proof that there is no God. It is something that happens in the natural course of life due to the brokenness of the world and the brokenness of our nature. Suffering occurs because our intellect and will are disordered and our bodies are prone to decay and death. Sometimes suffering occurs because we make bad choices. Other times it results from the bad choices of others. God does not necessarily desire that we suffer, but he always desires that we grow closer to him through our suffering.

Hope is always needed, especially in times of suffering. Hope is what gets us through these times. Hope assures us of the merit of suffering—the ability to unite our suffering to the suffering of Christ as a means of growing closer to Christ and as a prayer for others. Hope also reminds us that our

---

[1] Leo J. Trese, *The Faith Explained* (Philippines: Sinag-Tala, 1983), p. 106.

suffering will end. We will not suffer forever. Rather, hope assures us that we are not made for suffering, but destined for eternal joy.

While we suffer, it can be hard to feel hopeful. This is natural. Yet, it is comforting to know that God is intimately aware of our despair. In our times of despair, he reaches out to us and begs us to make even the simplest act of hope, whether that be "Jesus, I hope in you even though I feel like I have no hope," or "Jesus, help me to hope in you because I feel nothing." God will respond to such acts of hope! He will give us the hope we need to endure. To cry out in hope, when we feel no hope whatsoever, is, in fact, the greatest act of hope.

To live in hope, it is imperative that we persevere in prayer. We must pray in order to maintain a relationship with God who is the source of our hope. We must also specifically pray that God increases our hope.

Prayer is a dialogue with God—a constant reminder of God's involvement in our lives and a constant striving to grow closer to God. Prayer focuses us on God who is the source of and reason for our hope. Through prayer, our hope is strengthened as we draw closer to the font of hope.

Regular prayer becomes a habit—a habit that carries us through the times when our strength fails us. If we regularly get up early and exercise, we will find it much easier to do so at times when we are tired, lazy, or otherwise tempted to stay in bed. For even the most devout, prayer can be very challenging during times of great suffering. For us to persevere in prayer during such times, it is necessary that we are well acquainted with prayer—that prayer is our natural routine; that we engage in prayer constantly, almost without even having to think about it.

We must specifically pray for hope. We must ask God to increase hope within us. And we should petition God for increased hope not only in times of suffering, but also when things are going well. We often pray for an increase of faith and constantly ask for greater love, but how often do we pray for the gift of hope? Perhaps that is why the world is so full of despair. We should remember that hope is the virtue that brings the greatest happiness. We must never take hope for granted; we must constantly ask our Lord for more hope.

We are encouraged by St. Paul to always rejoice in hope. We must rejoice in hope during both good and bad times. In the good times, we must rejoice in gratitude. We must practice hope lest we take the gift of hope for granted. We must acknowledge that God is the source of all good things, rejoicing in the realization that God has given us so many good things here on earth as a taste of the perfection that awaits us in Heaven. We must also practice hope in good times as a reminder that no matter how good things appear now, this is nothing compared to what God has prepared for us in our eternal future.

In the bad times, we must rejoice in hope, despite our doubt and pain. We must rejoice because this is when hope is most needed. It is in suffering that we must live hope most abundantly and remind ourselves that Jesus has conquered the world. All sin and pain will come to an end because of the victory won for us by Christ on the Cross. We are destined for the glory of eternal life in Heaven.

Hope in Despair

We have acknowledged the fact that God gives us reason to hope, no matter what. Even in the dark, challenging times, we are called to turn to God and live in hope. But hope is not always easy to live. All of us will, at some point in our lives, find ourselves deep in despair.

How are we to remain hopeful when faced with financial ruin, serious personal illness, or the death of a loved one? How can we hope as our family faces eviction or our child is diagnosed with cancer? How are we to hope in God when one of his representatives on earth has betrayed our trust and caused us immense pain? It's not easy and no one should feel ashamed of the natural tendency to despair, but we must resist this temptation. And we must fight for the very hope that we do not even feel.

In the depths of despair, we must remind ourselves of the truth that God loves us. And true love requires freedom. Therefore, in love, God allows—but does not desire—the terrible consequences of sin. We must not blame God for evil in the world. We must not blame God for the suffering we experience. Neither evil nor suffering negates the truth that God loves us.

God loves us in the depths of our pain and despair. He loves us despite whether or not we feel his love. God continues to love us even though others hurt us. God loves us despite the fact that we have some genetic anomaly or have fallen victim to some natural disaster. God loves us even when sin causes us great pain. God loves us so much that he became man in order to share in all of our suffering. In the Garden and on the Cross, Jesus was emptied of the Father's consolation. As a human, Jesus experienced utter despair. Jesus freely walked into the depths of our darkness so that we could always look to him to lead us back out into the light.

God never abandons us. God is in our suffering just as he is in our joy. Our feeling of abandonment does not change this reality. If God truly abandoned us, we would cease to exist. Every moment God animates us. We are because God is and because God desires us to be. His loving gaze is fixed on us every instant. He could not be more concerned about us. In God's eyes, every one of us is the most important human alive; every one of us is his most beloved child.

In times of greatest despair, we must remember that hope is more a choice than a feeling. We must choose to hope. We must pray for the gift of hope. We must cry out to God from the depths of our despair. Then we must live in hope, regardless of our feelings.

Hope in Death

It is sometimes said that from the moment we are born, we begin to die. What a foolish statement. In fact, from the moment we die we begin to truly live! Death is not the end, but a new beginning. Death is not the failure of life, but its completion and perfection.

In death, we leave behind all that is limited, imperfect, and unsatisfying. We leave a world broken and disordered by sin, subject to disease and death. Death is the means by which our bodies are resurrected and the world is recreated. Through death, we enter into a glorious life in Heaven. Death is the means by which we are united fully with God, never to be separated again. Death is the necessary step by which we leave confusion for knowledge, sadness for joy, separation for unity, mortality for eternity, brokenness for completeness, desire for satiation, and potential for realization. From the moment we are born, we begin not to die, but to prepare for eternal life.

Despite this truth about death, it is normal to fear death and to feel great sadness when a loved one dies. It is natural to fear death because despite what we know about it, we have not yet experienced it. On this side of death, we cannot fully grasp the ecstasy that awaits us on the other side. It is also understandable to feel sadness when a loved one dies. Regardless of our hope for their eternal joy and for our eventual reunion, we can no longer experience the physical presence of this person in our lives. There is an absence where once there was a very important person. It is natural to despair in the face of death. But it is also natural to hope.

Remember what we acknowledged very early in this book: By definition, God is infinite and fully complete; he does not need anything. He did not create us to amuse him or to give him love or provide him with anything that he lacked. Rather, God created us to give himself to us. He created us to share in his love and happiness forever. God created us not for death, but for life—true, perfect eternal life with him.

Jesus assured us that death was not the end. He promised that eternal life awaited all who accepted his salvation. He assured us of the joy of Heaven. And Jesus did not just talk about the resurrection that followed death. He proved it.

Jesus died. He rose from the dead. And Jesus revealed to his followers the glory of the Resurrection.

The convincing witness of Jesus's Resurrection is seen in the lives of the Apostles. While Jesus lived, he was obviously a very impressive person. He spoke movingly, lived heroically, and performed incredible miracles. And these acts of Jesus had quite an effect on the Apostles. They left their families, jobs, and everything they knew to follow him—until things got rough—and then they abandoned him.

Despite everything Jesus said and did during his life, it was not enough for his timid followers to overcome doubt and fear. While Jesus was still alive, they were afraid to stand with him against the leaders of their people. While Jesus was still alive, they couldn't even find the courage to admit they knew him. But, after Jesus died, they fearlessly engaged not only the Jewish leaders, but also the very might of the Roman Empire. They proclaimed Jesus to anyone and everyone they met, even those who would torture and kill them for it. And they died in the absolute hope of Heaven.

What changed these simple followers of Jesus? How did men with no apparent leadership or oratory skills decide to change the entire world? What gave them the ability to not only overcome the fear of death, but to lovingly embrace it? Why was their witness so compelling to others? Why do we even today follow their example and embrace the same hope? They witnessed the resurrected Christ!

St. Paul, who was not one of the first Twelve Apostles and might never have even seen Jesus during Jesus's life, poignantly noted that if Christ did not truly rise from the dead, his faith and everyone's faith in Jesus was completely worthless. Yet, in faith and hope, he withstood more persecution for his witness than many of the other Apostles. And St. Paul joyfully embraced martyrdom. Why? Because Christ truly rose from the dead!

If Christ had not risen, we would have no reason for hope. If Christ had not risen, we should fear our own death and despair in the loss of others. But Christ *is* risen! He has triumphed over death. He has overcome death once and for all. So, in hope, we may exalt in the words of St. Paul, "Death is swallowed up in victory. Where, O death, is your victory? Where, O death, is your sting?" (1 Cor 15:54–55).

SEVEN

Mary, Mother of Hope

Literally (Sound Familiar?)

For the same reason that Mary is literally the Mother of Mercy, she is also literally the Mother of Hope. Mary bore Hope within her womb and gave birth to Hope. Mary was given the singular grace to be the Mother of God, our Lord and Savior Jesus Christ.

God chose Mary above all other women to be the New Eve. From Eve came sin and death; from Mary came redemption and life. Eve rebelled against God and mankind was expelled from the Garden of Eden; Mary submitted completely to the will of God and the gates of Heaven were opened. Through the defiance of Eve, despair entered the world; through the compliance of Mary, hope returned.

In the Father's great love for us, he sent his Son to redeem us from our sin, reunite us to God, and glorify our human natures in order that we might be able to fully partake in the Divine Life. God wished to restore, as man, the hope lost by man. Hence, God chose to become fully human. The Son of God was born of woman. It was within Mary's womb that Jesus was formed. From Mary's flesh, Jesus received his flesh.

Being born of Mary, the second Person of the Holy Trinity assumed completely and inseparably a human nature in addition to his divine nature. In this, Heaven was wedded to earth and mankind was given the hope of Heaven.

Jesus took upon himself all of our sins and failings. He freely chose to share in our pain and sorrow. He paid the debt owed to God that we were unable to pay. Jesus redeemed our human nature broken by sin—not merely restoring it to its original state, but glorifying it by his divine nature.

For all eternity God foresaw the unique beauty of Mary. From the moment of her conception, God preserved her from the stain of sin, as he did Eve. But Mary, unlike Eve or any other human, subjugated her will completely to that of God. She said yes to God in all things. And for this God chose Mary to be the Mother of Hope.

Mary, Ever Hopeful

Mary is our great example of hope. From the moment of her conception until her Assumption into Heaven, Mary embraced this virtue. She was faced with many trials and underwent great suffering, but Mary never gave in to despair. Rather, she trusted in God completely and always surrendered to the divine will. Mary's words at the Annunciation were the words ever on her lips, "*Fiat!*"—"Thy will be done!"

The Annunciation. While Mary was betrothed to Joseph, but not yet living with him, an angel appeared to her and announced that she would give birth. As Mary had taken a vow to God to remain a perpetual virgin, this announcement was undoubtedly perplexing to her.[1] In response to Mary's humble affirmation of her vow to God, the angel responded that she would remain a virgin and that she would conceive through the power of God (cf. Lk 1:34–35). Unable to fully understand what God had in store for her and not knowing how Joseph would react to her pregnancy (accusing her of adultery and having her stoned was certainly a possibility), Mary said, "Behold, I am the handmaid of the Lord. May it be done to me according to your word" (Lk 1:38).

Like all of us, Mary possessed free will. She was given a choice to say yes or no to God. God's will for her at that moment must have seemed rather scary. She faced the very real possibility of being condemned as an adulteress and stoned to death. Yet, Mary trusted in God's plan, and she hoped. Mary's hope was rewarded: Joseph did not condemn her, but lovingly took Mary into his home and became the adopted father of her son.

The Birth of Jesus. Mary experienced all of the unexpected and seemingly unfortunate twists of life. Because of the Roman census, Mary spent her last days of pregnancy journeying to Bethlehem. Because of the overcrowded conditions there, she was forced to give birth to Jesus in a stable—a rather inauspicious entrance for a child who, as the angel had declared to Mary, would sit on the throne of King David, rule over the Israelites, and be called the Son of God. Mary accepted all these things without ever losing hope. The

---

[1] The tradition of the Church teaches that Mary made a vow of perpetual virginity even before the Annunciation. Cf., e.g., St. Augustine, *De sancta virginitate*, 4.

Old Testament prophecies were fulfilled and God's will was accomplished.

The Presentation and Finding in the Temple. In keeping with the Jewish Law, Jesus was presented in the Temple forty days after his birth. As Mary's firstborn, he was dedicated to God. Like the pride and joy we feel as we bring our children to the font of Baptism, this should have been a joyous occasion, filled with hope for Jesus's future. Instead, it was a revelation of the pain and sacrifice that awaited Mary. Simeon revealed to her that Jesus would bring great division in Israel and that Mary would suffer immensely—her heart would be "pierced with a sword"—for the good of us all (cf. Lk 2:22–38).

At the moment Mary was giving her son to his true Father ritually in the Temple, the Father was revealing his plan of salvation, which involved the sacrifice of his Only-Begotten Son for all. Jesus was to be rejected by his people. He was to be condemned. Jesus was to be tortured and crucified. And Mary was to witness all of this. She was to share in her son's agony. As his heart would be pierced with a lance—physically—her heart would be pierced with a sword—spiritually.

Mary was given a small taste of the future when Jesus was twelve. She and Joseph took Jesus to the Temple in Jerusalem for the Feast of Passover. One day into the return journey, Mary and Joseph learned that Jesus was not among their extended family with whom they traveled. They returned immediately, and found Jesus in the Temple three days later.

For three days, Mary was forced to live in hope that her son would be alive and free from harm. She had to hope completely in God to take care of Jesus. Mary had to avoid blaming herself or Joseph (for they bore no fault). Upon finding Jesus, Mary sought to understand the will of God, asking Jesus, "Son, why have you done this to us? Your father and I have been looking for you with great anxiety" (Lk 2:48). God desired, however, that Mary would continue to live not in complete understanding or consolation, but in hope. Jesus responded, "Why were you looking for me? Did you not know that I must be in my Father's house?" (Lk 2:49).

Mary did not despair or rebel after these experiences. She did not say to God, "This is too much for me to bear." Rather, she embraced God's plan. Pondering and praying, Mary "kept all these things in her heart" (Lk 2:51). Mary walked forward to her designated end, holding onto hope.

The Passion and Death of Jesus. The height of hope, in Mary, is seen during the Passion and Death of her son. Jesus, who would be king of Israel, was rejected by his people and condemned by their leaders. He, who would sit on a throne, was tied to a pillar and scourged mercilessly. He, who would be king, was crowned with thorns. Yet, Mary trusted and hoped.

If we ever doubt God's love for us and begin to lose hope because of some suffering we have to endure, we must look to Mary. God loved her more than any other and chose her to be the mother of his Son, yet she had to witness the unimaginable torture and death of her son. She beheld his flesh shredded by the whips, his face beaten and spit upon, his strength spent under the weight of the Cross, his hands and feet pierced. Mary who once held the swaddled divine infant to her breast in a manger now held the naked and broken corpse of her beloved son. Yet, the words in Mary's heart at the Cross were the same as those on her lips at the Annunciation, "*Fiat!*"—"Thy will be done!"

Mary endured all, in love. Even as her heart was breaking, she never despaired. She trusted completely in God; she hoped. And Mary's hope was not in vain. Her son rose from the dead. By his suffering, Jesus redeemed all of mankind and won for us all the hope of Heaven. Because of the depth of her hope, God entrusted Mary with the honor of being mystically united to Jesus's suffering—a level of intimacy short only of the Trinity itself. And Mary was rewarded for her hope: she was assumed body and soul into Heaven where she was crowned Queen of Heaven and Earth.

Help Me Mamma

As "Mediatrix of Grace" and constant intercessor to Our Lord on our behalf, Mary is our ally in hope. She desires that we live every moment in hope. Yet, Mary recognizes how challenging this can be. She shares our humanity and understands our doubts. Therefore, Mary is devoted to pleading unceasingly that we might be given the grace from her Son to persevere in hope to the end.

Before he died, Jesus gave us Mary to be our mother. Mary obediently accepted this role and lovingly undertook it. Mary embraced the Apostles as their mother after the death of Jesus. She forgave those who abandoned her son, gathered them together, and cared for them. She also prayed for them. Mary continued to be a source of strength for them both here on earth and after she was assumed into Heaven.

We could not ask for a better intercessor for hope. Mary is our mother. She loves us. She wants what is best for us. She desires that we know that we are destined for eternal joy, united forever with her Son. She wants us to be hopeful here on earth and fulfilled completely in Heaven. She will never turn her back on us. She will never ignore our needs. Rather, she will unceasingly plead our cause before the throne of God if we but ask for her help.

The Hail Holy Queen, which is prayed at the end of the Rosary, addresses Mary, "Hail, holy Queen, Mother of Mercy, our life, our sweetness and *our hope.*" In this prayer, we recognize that God has enthroned Mary as Queen of all. As Queen of earth, Mary is intimately concerned with the wellbeing of us, her children. As Queen of Heaven, Mary has been given the special power of pleading on our behalf before the King.

As the Mother of Mercy, Mary is necessarily the Mother of Hope. As Mary has the ability to obtain mercy for us from God, it is only fitting that we should be filled with hope. Mary *will* intercede for us. God *will* grant her request. God *will* shower mercy upon us. We *will* reach Heaven.

Our Lady, Mother of Hope,

Pray for us!

Conclusion

Jesus, I Trust in You!

When our Lord revealed the Image of Divine Mercy to St. Faustina, he instructed that it be signed with the words "Jesus, I trust in you!" In this phrase, our Lord reveals the interconnectedness of hope and mercy. The ultimate mercy here on earth is the gift of hope, and the eternal gift of mercy is the consummation of hope.

In saying "Jesus, I trust in you," we are in effect saying, "Jesus, I hope in your mercy." Since we cannot merit Heaven, we can never hope to attain Heaven without God's mercy. But we trust that God will be merciful, and so we have hope. Since we trust in God's mercy, we have the reasonable expectation that we will attain Heaven.

God is so merciful. He has shown his mercy by giving us life and all of creation for our enjoyment. God shows his mercy by constantly forgiving us our sins. But the greatest mercy God gives to us here on earth is his promise that he has prepared a place for us in Heaven, and that this place is ours for the asking. In hope, we are assured that no matter how grave our sins, God is willing to forgive them. In hope, we are assured that no matter how much suffering we endure during our life's journey, Heaven will be worth it. In fact, in hope, we are assured that even the joy we experience here on earth will be magnified infinitely in Heaven.

God's final act of mercy toward us will be his eternal gift of mercy at the end of our lives. If we have called upon his mercy in life, God will be merciful to us in death. His merciful judgment will be the final forgiveness of all sin and our glorification in Heaven. In this final act of mercy we will realize our hope.

"Jesus, I trust in you!" is as much our acclamation of hope as it is our mantra of mercy. Let us use these words in recognition that God *is* Mercy and Hope! When we are steeped in sin and in need of mercy, let us beg God with the words, "Jesus, I trust in you!" When we are broken in doubt and falling into despair, let us cry out to God, "Jesus, I trust in you!" When our spirits soar in awe of God's mercy, let us thank him with the words, "Jesus, I trust in you!" When we are overwhelmed with the realization of the joy that awaits us in Heaven, let us praise God with the words, "Jesus, I trust in you!"

ONE YEAR.
20 MINUTES A DAY.

Encounter the Power and
Wonder of God's Word with
Bible in a Year. The simple
format guides you through all
73 books of the Bible in just one year.

Learn more at **CatholicBibleInAYear.com**

RESPONDING TO RELATIVISM

WITH LOGIC AND LOVE.

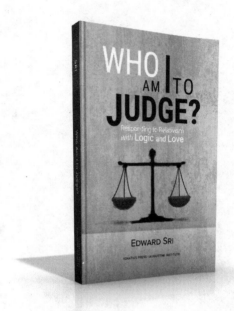

WHO AM I TO JUDGE?

DR. EDWARD SRI·

In an age in which preference has replaced morality, many people find it difficult to speak the truth, afraid of the reactions they will receive if they say something is right or wrong. Using engaging stories and personal experience, Dr. Sri helps us understand the classical view of morality and equips us to engage relativism, appealing to both the head and the heart.